T0330169

Africa Must Be Modern

Africa Must Be Modern

A Manifesto

Olúfẹ́mi Táíwò

INDIANA UNIVERSITY PRESS

BLOOMINGTON & INDIANAPOLIS

This book is a publication of

Indiana University Press
Office of Scholarly Publishing
Herman B Wells Library 350
1320 East 10th Street
Bloomington, Indiana 47405 USA

iupress.indiana.edu

Telephone   800-842-6796
Fax   812-855-7931

Africa Must Be Modern: The Modern Imperative in Contemporary Africa,
A Manifesto © 2011 by Olúfẹ́mi Táíwò. Publishing rights licensed from
the original publisher, BOOKCRAFT LTD, Ibadan, Nigeria.

© 2014 by Olúfẹ́mi Táíwò
All rights reserved

Manufactured in the United States of America

Library of Congress Cataloging-in-Publication Data

Olúfẹ́mi Táíwò
Africa must be modern : a manifesto/ Olúfẹ́mi Táíwò—U.S. edition.
pages cm.—
Originally published: Ibadan, Nigeria : Bookcraft, 2011.
Includes index.
ISBN 978-0-253-01272-2 (cloth : alk. paper)—ISBN 978-0-253-01275-3 (pbk : alk.
paper)—ISBN 978-0-253-01278-4 (ebook) 1. Civilization, Modern. 2. Philosophy,
African. 3. Africa—Civilization. 4. Africa—Economic policy. 5. Africa—Social conditions.
6. Africa—Social life and customs. 7. Africa—Politics and government. I. Title.
DT14 .T343 2014
960.33—dc23
2013039900

1 2 3 4 5   19 18 17 16 15 14

For
Adéyínká Táíwò

Contents

Preface to the U.S. Edition

I am gratified that this little book is being republished for the North American audience after its original publication in Nigeria by a Nigerian publisher. Its publication in Nigeria fulfilled my original plan for the book as it began to take shape. My objective was to open a dialogue with African interlocutors who know the terrain of which this book treats quite intimately and who can easily, without translation, find their lives—personal, professional, cultural, political—reflected in the case that it makes. That it was a Nigerian publisher who put the book out was the luck of the draw for me: all I wanted was to put it out in the African continent.

In addition to the need for a conversation with my fellow African labourers in the search for lasting solutions to Africa's multifarious problems, I was also concerned that this not become another exile product, easily available to the privileged audience that I have here in North America, but hardly within reach of those whose lives, were its injunctions to be heeded, would be most impacted by the ensuing changes. As the reader will find out presently, this is not a book to burnish my academic or professional reputation. It is a fighting book and the fight has to be located in the appropriate theatre, not prosecuted from a distance.

Àrùn tí ń ṣe ogójì ní ń ṣe ọ̀ọ́dúnrún; àrùn tí ńṣe Abóyadé, gbogbo olóya ní ń ṣe. [What ails forty is what ails three hundred; what afflicts Abóyadé is an affliction shared by all of Ọya's adherents.] So goes a Yorùbá proverb. This manifesto demands that Africa be modern. If there is anything that ails modernity, it goes without saying that the same ailment would afflict Africa were it to become modern. At the present moment, the book argues, what ails modernity is of less relevance to Africa than what recommends it. Modernity is, historically speaking, a global phenomenon. In asking that Africa embrace modernity, we already assume that there is a lack in the African life space and that Africa could be made better, and definitely not worse, by becoming more like the countries that are considered modern at the present time. This is not to suggest that modernity and the societies that embody its core tenets are without blemish. If there is something untoward happening to existing modern countries, we can be sure that Africa will be well served by steering clear of such pitfalls as it advances towards realizing modernity. Simultaneously, those who are already modern might learn from our laser-like focus on its merits what is missing from their realisation of modernity or how current circumstances chip away from or grossly distort modernity's tenets in their institutions, processes, and practices. I do argue momentarily that modernity is under such pressures in current American society. This is the ultimate illumination that this book promises to my North American readers and readers outside Africa.

When I wrote this manifesto, its relevance to the North American context was the furthest thing from my mind. But my friend, Rick Simonson, was the first to suggest to me that, on his reading of the original manuscript, there might be some resonance in the American situation for the book. He was right. And the opportunity of this republication has focused my mind firmly on the object of his prescience.

Given my experience with working on modernity in a North American context in the course of more than two decades, I do not exaggerate when I say that for some time there—definitely in the nineties of the last century—many thought that modernity was passé. It wasn't just that this view was prevalent in the academy and in the scholarship that dominated that period. Of greater importance, still, is the fact that among intellectuals and ordinary folk alike being modern is so pervasive that it seems like first nature to them. That is, it should come as no surprise that North Americans take modernity for granted. For most people, this is the only reality that they know. That life could be led otherwise than in the modern register is not something that is ever before their mind. That there are other-than-modern ways of being human often sounds like a discovery to generations of first-year students that I have been privileged to teach at different American institutions during my ongoing study of modernity.

Because modernity is life, it is easy for those whose life it is to regard it as natural and, better still, take it for granted. It may be that being an ex-colonised, especially that special breed of ex-colonised that is the African, I have always been acutely aware of the best and worst of modernity in both its philosophical discourse and its practical manifestations. The denial of its benefits to Africans, the delivery of which colonialism promised them as recompense for bearing its burdens while colonialism lasted, inspired me to look at how those benefits might be redeemed for Africa's long-suffering peoples. In making the case for the continuing relevance, make that necessity, of modernity in any discussion of Africa's future prospects, I had to strip down modernity to its barest core. In so doing, it became very clear that, given their familiarity with it, the contempt with which many in North America treat modernity leaves them vulnerable to the effects of the despotic inroads that are being made at the present time on the benefits of modernity and its associated principles of social ordering and modes of social living.

The contempt for modernity, bred by their familiarity with it, has made Americans, especially, become unmindful of the tyrannical distortions that have begun to mark the evolution of modern institutions, processes, and practices that structure their quotidian lives. On this score, Americans need be reminded that at no other time in recent history than now is it truer to claim that "the price of liberty is eternal vigilance." Although few people may now think that this admonition is relevant at the present time in the United States, I beg to differ.

Here is why. One can point to the growing assault on one of the fundaments of modernity: the legal system. Over the course of the last thirty years, the protections offered the legal subject—the centrepiece of the modern legal system, if there be any—have come under ferocious attack by a Supreme Court that has aligned itself more and more with politicians and parts of the population that are more anxious for security than they are for liberty; more interested in revenge and retribution than they are in rehabilitation; more inclined to demonize offenders and prefer incarceration than in identifying the causes of crime and criminal behavior and fixing them. The draconian three-strikes laws in many jurisdictions do not entertain any distinctions between minor and major crimes, especially from the ranks of the minority populations in the United States, who may be incarcerated for life on third strikes that ordinarily would have attracted no more than slaps on the wrist in the past. The United States has now become the number one country with the highest incarceration rate in the world. Why more people do not see this as an unacceptable erosion of the foundation in liberty of the United States is for me a scandal. Worse still is the rightward shift in the Supreme Court that has made its majority become more amenable to attenuating the demands of the equal protection doctrine regarding unlawful search and seizure by the state and its agents in police departments across the land.

At the same time as the apex court has been complicit in the erosion of individual liberties, the legal system itself has been under attack for hewing closely to one of the core tenets of modernity: the priority of rules to outcomes. Many are those in the American population, especially on the right, who are convinced that, with its commitment to rules, the legal system has been letting off the guilty on technicalities. When you add this sense of injury to the explicit undermining, expressed in name calling and public damning of particular judges for not "enforcing the law," of the judiciary by many right-wing politicians—I am deliberately ignoring the toxic fulminations that are the staples of talk radio and other media—one should not be surprised at the violence, up to and including murder, directed at federal judges in recent years. Needless to say, those who persist in believing in the guilt of the accused otherwise found innocent by the legal system either do not understand the philosophical underpinnings of the modern legal system or have chosen to ignore them for political advantage. However that may be, continual querying of the theoretical underpinnings of the modern legal system bodes ill for the future of modernity in this society, too.

Closely related to the goings-on in the legal sphere are even more egregious outcomes in the political sphere. The 2012 election cycle should give a cause for pause for all those who are desirous of seeing modernity continue to be the guiding principle of thought and life in the United States. Again the signs are ominous. We have now in many states of the union governors and lawmakers who are more interested in curbing the control American women have over their bodies and, by so doing, abridging the individualism as well as its philosophical principle of subjectivity that are the hallmarks of modernity.

In addition to the assault on women's rights and associated rights regarding same-sex marriage, we have in many states that are controlled by right-wing politicians the proliferation of behavior that mimics those of tin-pot dictators of old in banana republics for whom law is merely an extension of their power to realise their will, principles be damned! We have laws made in Kentucky and Mississippi targeted at sole subjects, for example particular abortion facilities, that, in so doing, violate the requirement that laws be general and universal in their scope. The administrations in Pennsylvania, Michigan, Wisconsin, South Carolina, Ohio, and Virginia all made attempts—frustrated by the courts—to make thinly disguised election rules to disenfranchise the other party's voters and enhance their chances of winning with even fewer percentages of the registered electorate. In Arizona, Ohio, and Florida, voting literature, including ballots, containing the wrong dates for elections were sent to certain segments—blacks and Hispanics, for the most part. And in Ohio and Florida, their respective administrations worked valiantly to expand early voting opportunities in areas populated by their partisans while simultaneously assiduously working to limit early voting in opposition-dominated areas.

In the aftermath of the elections, some of the states mentioned above are in the process of altering the formula for awarding the electoral votes, by which American presidents are really elected in the electoral college, in order to institutionalise the possible repeated elections of Republican party candidates who fail and, it seems increasingly to be the case, cannot win the popular vote for president. Might military coups be too far off when white people stop being the majority of the United States population a few decades hence? If indeed the price of liberty is eternal vigilance, it is way past time for Americans to become more agitated by the despotic inroads into the evolution of modernity in their country.

So far, I have talked of those segments of the American population for whom being modern is a banal fact. But it is by no means the case that modernity has the same resonance for all segments of the population. Many political groups as well as religious ones have different kinds of problems with modernity. The leadership of the Catholic Church and diverse evangelical denominational groups, including the black church, have differing degrees of unease with the implications of the modern tenet of individualism when it comes to matters of abortion, same-sex marriage, and Church-State relations.

There is yet another segment of the population whose relationship to and experience of modernity calls for comment in our discussion. Generations of immigrants have followed the path of the original settlers and have come to North America for "life, liberty, and the pursuit of happiness." Yet, it is clear that the relationship between older and more recently arrived immigrants is often conflicted, and we may make more sense of some of the conflicts between immigrants and host communities in terms of their divergent understandings of the tenets of modernity. This is usually what is meant when host communities insist that recent immigrants embrace the founding principles of "our country." The irony is often lost on such claimants of orthodoxy how much latitude modernity allows and how much responsibility it places on individuals in constructing their respective selves.

In addition to these conflicted understandings between host and immigrant communities are the serious conflicts internal to different immigrant communities themselves. Many new immigrants are, with good reasons, wedded to their original cultural understandings. But they end up raising what are essentially, culturally speaking, American children, many of whom find absolutely incomprehensible many of the ways in which their parents represent to them the embodiment of the old ways. From arranged marriages to so-called honor killings to identity politics, many are the points of friction promised by modernity's core tenets, especially that of individualism and the rule of law. And we should not forget how continuing racism, especially of the institutional variety, represents a subversion of the promise of modernity for nonwhite Americans in their experience of life in North America.

It is my hope that this book reminds my North American audience of the legacy of modernity of which they are inheritors, of the centrality of its core tenets to the life that they have come to take for granted and of the many threats to these advantages at the present time posed by those who promise no better future but a reversal of the progress that the modern age represents in the annals of human history. Even though I believe that the best life for humans cannot be delivered by the best realisation of modernity and its tenets, we must never forget or take lightly how much progress modernity is for humanity and continues to be. Of that my conviction remains unshakable.

I owe Dee Mortensen, my editor at Indiana University Press, a debt of gratitude for adopting this book for publication in the United States. She is a joy to work with, and the same goes for her team at the press. I am grateful.

Olúfẹ́mi Táíwò
Africana Studies and Research Center
Cornell University
Ithaca, NY
September 8, 2013

Acknowledgments

This book has been a long time coming. It originated from my desire to make sense of my place in the scheme of things where putting my intellectual training to use is concerned. For as long as I can remember, I have always been exercised by the prostrate position of Africans in the world, beginning in Ibadan, Nigeria, where I was born and raised. I have always felt shamed by human suffering wherever in the world it occurs. And if there has been a single thread that has supplied the unifying theme of my life so far, it is this: to help birth a world in which poverty, ill-health, and ignorance no longer have a place and all humans possess and are enabled to exercise that freedom that undergirds the dignity that pertains to our status as humans.

I have lived all my life seeing this freedom denied and humanity battered even as it is made poor, illiterate, and unhealthy all across the African continent. I grew up in the early years of Nigeria's independence and was conscious enough to witness, even if I could not fully understand then, the propagation in political campaigns and in various mass media of the lofty ideals of freedom and a better and more humane life that had driven the struggle for Nigeria's independence. My studies would later make me more acutely aware of the failure to realise those dreams in various places in the continent; a failure that has multiple authors—politicians, business persons, leaders of various stripes, and, most significantly, intellectuals.

This book represents my attempt to offer one way of moving forward that is distilled from my reading of history, philosophy, economics, and other disciplines as they have been put to the service of liberating humanity in different parts of the world. In a sense, therefore, many friends, acquaintances, students, teachers, comrades, opponents, and others, whose paths it has been my fate to cross and intersect with over time, have contributed to the case made in this manifesto. Simultaneously, none but I should be held responsible for its contents. Aware as I am of how much the case made in the following pages riles many in the global African context, especially in the continent, I have, over the course of the time that it has taken to complete the manuscript, refrained from sharing portions of the manuscript with my usual group of interlocutors, dear friends, who would otherwise have read it and saved me from all the follies it contains. I simply did not wish for any one of them to be guilty by association or accused of not restraining me from going ahead with what might turn out to be utter folly. I can only hope that whatever folly it represents is instructive and illuminating.

Dear reader, in light of what I just said, please resist any and every temptation to hold responsible for any of the views in this book any of the people that I now proceed to acknowledge hereunder. Adéyínká Táíwò often was a one-person audience for many of the snippets that later became significant parts of the text. She has more than earned its dedication. Saheed Yinka Adejumobi comes a close second to being a captive audience for many formulations that now populate the book. Tejumola Olaniyan and Kunle Ajibade weighed in at crucial stages in the development of the work. Tunde Bewaji provided me with a foretaste of how some might react to its central claims. Catherine McKinley provided crucial advice on where this might fit in my exile journey. I hope someday to write the book she thinks I should write for my American audience. When there is life, there is hope. Mawuena Logan and Lisa Aubrey, at different times, and independently of each other, forced more clarity on me than they realised. Rick Simonson provided much encouragement regarding the relevance of the work beyond Africa's borders. I thank them all.

Bankole Olayebi, my publisher, deserves gratitude and not just for publishing the book. He never hesitated to adopt the book for his imprint and he has been a very enthusiastic promoter of it. I look forward to more great conversations with him. I am thankful that he is the manuscript's primary publisher: I did not want it published outside the continent.

Finally, I would like to thank my friend and colleague, Professor Heisook Kim, of the Department of Philosophy and Scranton College at Ewha Womans University, Seoul, Korea. It was she who arranged for me to spend part of my Sabbatical Leave at their institution in Fall Semester 2008. The time I spent there was critical to the writing of some sections of the book. My home institution, Seattle University, provided me with the opportunity of the Sabbatical Leave in 2008/09 during which I completed the first full draft of the book. I am grateful to both institutions for their support.

Seattle, USA
February 16, 2011

Introduction

The thesis of this book is very simple and straightforward: there is nothing that is wrong with Africa at the present time that a serious engagement with and acceptance of modernity cannot solve or, at least, contribute to solving. I argue in what follows: Africa must be modern. Let me say it again: Africa must be modern. And it must be modern NOW; not tomorrow; not in the near future; not in the far future. Of course, I know that all the nay-saying nativists, the do-nothing, "let's find an African solution to our problem" advocates, the pseudo-anti-Western-imperialism crowd, the renegade rump of anti-neo-colonialist noisemakers, will gang up to denounce what is proposed in this manifesto. There will be no shortage of comrades who will stop at nothing to paint me a turncoat, a fifth columnist, a pseudo-Marxist, a running dog of imperialism, a capitalist quisling, and what have you. I have a simple response to them: you are very welcome.

To them I say: you do not have to read this book. It is not directed at the likes of you. By the same token, if you are one of those in the African world who believe that being modern is synonymous with being Western, this book is not for you and you may be too close-minded to benefit from the discussion to follow. Whatever I say in the rest of the book is not designed to break through the fortress of your mind. For one thing, you are wrong in your estimation and reading this might actually persuade you of your error; but, first, you have to be open to persuasion.

For the reader who is open to persuasion, who is willing to allow me to plead my cause, who is prepared to suspend judgment while I lay out the case for my clarion call to Africa and Africans, I am grateful. Even if you end up deciding that the journey laid out in this manifesto does not sway you to join in, I hope that you at least think that I have done a decent job of persuading you to take a good look at existing templates for moving Africa forward in the shortest possible time. That the task of making life more abundant in the continent, of turning the continent into a destination of choice for humanity looking for a better and more fulfilled life, a location where children are not press-ganged into navigating life's many rapids too soon in their lives, one marked by a horizon of possibilities for scientific discoveries, artistic and philosophical creations; in short, that the task of moving Africa to the 21st century not only cannot, it should and will not wait; rather it ought to have been completed in the last century.

Africa must be modern. Put simply, Africa must embrace individualism as a principle of social ordering; make reason central in its relation to, activity upon, understanding of, and producing knowledge about the world, both physical and social, that it inhabits; and adopt progress as its motto in all things. The position just stated is rarely encountered in discourse about, in and on the continent or its Diaspora. On the contrary, no thanks to the militancy and stridency of the nativists, those who wish to celebrate African genius at adapting the wisdom of others and, by so doing, domesticate modernity for the benefit of Africa, Africans, and their life and thought, are practically shouted to silence or, at best, limited to furtive expressions of their preference.

And there is no doubt that with the widespread diffusion of white supremacy in the world's relations with Africa, the roots of which can be traced to the slave trade and slavery as well as the peculiar form that colonialism took in Africa, it is almost required of an African intellectual that she or he be hostile to modernity and its suppositions. It is almost as if an African like me who deliberately embraces modernity as a way of life that promises at the present time a better template for remaking life and thought in Africa must be a dope; one who is suffering from pathological dependence on white people as well as a severe case of self-hatred. This charge, this awful name-calling, has managed, over the course of the last century, to silence many in the continent who would and could have been the spearhead of positive change for Africa's long-suffering peoples.

No doubt, much of the hostility towards modernity abroad in the continent is due to the conflicted nature of the relationship between Africans and modernity once colonialism was clamped on the continent. From then on, many Africans came to misidentify modernity with colonisation and westernisation and a plague-on-all-your-houses attitude sedimented in much of the continent towards modernity-as-colonisation-and-westernisation. Nevertheless, a solid familiarity with the true history of modernity in Africa shows that it predated colonialism in at least the Western part of the continent and that, long before colonialism came to hold sway, there was a handful of people in West Africa who had embraced Christian-inflected modernity and were eager to remake their lives and their societies in the modern image. These were the agents who gave fight to colonialism throughout the colonial period but a great number of whom soured on modernity as a consequence of the odious racialisation of life and discourse that framed and typified colonialism in the entire continent. The discourse of modernity in the continent is yet to recover from this tradition of hostility towards and disengagement from it.

It is time for us to separate from this tradition which, as the fate of the continent attests, has ill-served Africa. If any evidence be needed, all we need do is look at all the countries in Asia and Latin America that have shown the most remarkable improvements in their material and social lives. They all, without exception, have torn pages off the book of modernity, especially its economic component—capitalism—and left Africa behind in all areas of life. What is more, all of those countries—India, South Korea, Brazil, Indonesia, Malaysia, Singapore, Mexico—are ex-colonies. This means that being an ex-colony is no insurmountable barrier to building a modern economy and giving the old capitalist economies a good run for their money. Sadly, there is not a single country in Africa, with the exception of the only modern economy in the continent—South Africa—that can be listed among the industrialising economies of the world.

Although colonialism did not constitute an impediment to the development of the countries just referred to, we have to concede that in the case of Africa, colonialism was and, with its lingering effects, continues to be the bulwark against the possibility of Africans consciously laying hold of modernity and its myriad discourses and turning them to the service of restoring dignity to Africans through economic development and socio-political transformation.

Africa Must Be Modern

ONE

Why Africa Must Get on Board the Modernity Express

Our capacity for and evidence of self-deception on a mass scale regarding our relationship to modernity and its associated principles, practices, and processes is what has made me challenge us to come out and wrestle modernity's beast directly without ifs, buts, or other alibis.

THIS BOOK has a long and varied genesis. It all goes back to sometime in the spring of 1986. I was finishing my doctoral dissertation and generally preparing with supreme confidence and optimism for my repatriation to my home country, Nigeria, where I, alongside many other fellow Nigerian expatriates then sojourning in Toronto, Canada, in search of the proverbial Golden Fleece, hoped to put our newly acquired skills to building our homeland. When I refer to confidence and optimism I am neither exaggerating nor misstating our orientation then. If there was one thing that my cohort of Nigerian graduate students congregated at that time in Toronto shared, it was a determination to be the generation of African scholars that would breach the persistent outward-looking orientation of African intellectual production. We saw it as our duty to, and were convinced that we could, stem the tide that had swept us and a lot of others to various countries of Europe and North America in pursuit of graduate degrees. We were determined to go back to Nigeria and, through our research and teaching activities, create local intellectual traditions, domesticate our scholarship, and generally create an enabling environment that would make it superfluous for our young best and brightest to seek post-graduate training abroad, especially in the humanities and the social sciences.

Judging by our own experience, we saw that in Europe and North America, not only were we constrained by the cultural context in which we were studying, our options for themes, and the general support infrastructure for relevant and critical discourse, continuity of exchanges, and the possibility of creating and sustaining a ferment in which new conflicts, ideas, tropes, themes, and so on can be incubated were nonexistent in our country of study. No doubt, we acquired some sophisticated tools of our different disciplines—we were technically sound—yet, we could not in honesty deny that we were sophisticated cultural bastards. Why were we cultural bastards? For the most part, and I am talking mostly of social scientific and humanistic disciplines, our topics did not fit into the Canadian context: they could be of interest only to Canadian "African Studies." Those of us in a discipline like philosophy could claim parentage in the so-called Western tradition. But our exemplars and even our names make us a bad fit!

The situation was more complicated in my case. Here is why. Even before I left Nigeria, I had become a Marxist whose radicalism intermixed with pan-Africanist and black nationalist commitments. So, I did not go to Canada for graduate work with a view to merely secure a job or pursue a career in teaching and research. My sights were set much higher: my Canadian training was going to be a mere stop on the long journey to changing the world and creating the best society possible for humans on earth. Towards this end, both as an undergraduate and graduate student in Nigeria, I was an activist with quite a resumé. I had done my share of public agitation, speech making, even rabble rousing, all in the service of recreating Nigeria and, by extension, our world.

Canada spoilt it all for me. I arrived in Canada thinking that, as a capitalist country, it would model many of the ills that our Marxist minds had associated with capitalism: dire living for the working masses, wide inequities in the distribution of wealth, warehousing of poor people, and the like. What is more, it took me quite some time to wean myself from the persistent belief that Toronto must be doing an incredibly effective job of hiding away its slums. After all, how could there be a major metropolis in a capitalist polity that was lacking one of its essential ornaments: warehouses for its poor and underprivileged! It eventually dawned on me that what then had been part of the dream of a new world without slums in my imagination was the banal reality of quotidian existence for Torontonians. The effect of this discovery was devastating, but not in the way that, from what I have said so far, the reader might think.

What Toronto and, by extension, Canada did was to show me that although the regaining of paradise on earth—a leitmotif of all utopian thinking—may be marked more by aspiration than by realisation, one society (the Canadian) had, at a minimum, redeemed for its members a bit of that ideal: a big city with no slum, no open gutters, clean streets, efficient public utilities, an orderly citizenry, generalised access for all—including foreign students—to health care services, and, most importantly, a say in how they were ruled and not just at election time. It showed me what the human mind can do when it sets itself to it. It showed me that what was a mere dream when I was in Nigeria had become part of my reality in Canada. The question that kept bugging me throughout my stay in Canada was: if Canadians could build a country such as I had the good fortune to inhabit for five years, why couldn't Nigerians?

It is important how we answer this question. We have two options. The first is to assert a radical difference between Canadians and Nigerians such that what Canadians are able to do, Nigerians cannot. This has to do with their respective natures—the Canadian personality versus the Nigerian personality. This is the answer that is often asserted by racists and white supremacists. Africans are congenitally incapable of creating the kind of society that I lauded in Canada. The second answer is to look closely at the enabling principles that were operational in the context of Canadian history and which might be used to explain Canada's success and see whether the same principles are present in Nigeria. On the other hand, we look at the disabling principles operational in Nigeria in the context of Nigerian history which might be used to explain Nigeria's failure. Either way, we would end up with useful insights. I took the second route. I was consumed with the desire to learn how Canadians were able to attain the reality that was a dream for which so-called idealists like me were derided in Nigeria for daring to entertain.

This brings me to that time in spring 1986 when, in the solitude of my Toronto apartment, the question hit me respecting what I was going to do on my return to Nigeria after I would have concluded my studies. It was an epiphany. Like all epiphanies, I cannot point to any particular event, incident, discussion, encounter, or prompt that arrested my thought and forced my mind to entertain the following challenge: Now that you are headed back to Nigeria, how are you going to prosecute the struggle for a changed world in that corner of the globe? Are you going to go back and pick up where you left off: rallies, marches, symposia, press conferences, and the occasional confrontation with the state and its trigger-happy goons? Although these questions were not immediately provoked, they were not without remote antecedents in my Canadian journey.

As I progressed through my studies, it became clear to me and others of my cohort that a singular failing of African radicals, especially us Marxists, was that we had misconstrued the import of Karl Marx's Thesis XI on Feuerbach which stated: "Philosophers have merely interpreted the world in various ways; the point, however, is to change it." From the dearth of fundamental literature on diverse aspects of African life to a near total absence of Marxist and other radical texts on the African world, it had by then become clear to me that African leftists had been so consumed by their eagerness to change the world that they had forgotten to take the preparatory first step of interpreting it. In other words, leftist African intellectuals and those of us who were their students and were set to take our place as teachers and guides of the future brigade of world changers were engaged in an impossible task: we were trying to change a world that we barely understood. There and then I resolved that I would not go back to doing the same thing I used to do. I determined that I was going to do my best as an interpreter of the African world, one who would do research and write essays, reports, articles, etc., which would equip those who wish to change the world with left interpretations to aid their exertions. I cannot be the judge of how well I have done in that respect. But I can say with utmost confidence that this is the goal to which I have thus far dedicated my energies in the last twenty-five years of my scholarly life.

Over the years, I have focused on different spheres of that largely uninterpreted world. As far back as 1986, it was very clear to me that many left African scholars did not understand and, if they understood, did not take seriously how the global economy worked. In the period since then, we had the newly industrialising countries of Asia and Latin America prove false the Marxian orthodoxy that capitalism could not be built in the so-called periphery. We have witnessed ex-colonies with profiles less promising than those of major African countries becoming competitive players in the global market while Africa's fortunes became more decrepit with the passage of time. The demise of so-called "really existing socialism" in Central and Eastern Europe provoked a whole new scramble for places in the global capitalist economy and new challenges for socio-political theory respecting how to live and what being human entails. Again, because of our poverty of imagination, African scholars have fallen far behind the rest of the world in interpreting our world and clearing the path to change for the better for Africa's peoples.

Twenty-five years hence, and several exchanges and smaller epiphanies later, I have come to the realisation that my worries all revolve around one recurring theme: Africa's response to, engagement with, place in, experience of, and hostility to MODERNITY. Say what? Modernity? Yes, modernity, the word, the idea, the movement, and so on. How did I come to this pass? Over time I have discovered that many of the issues that ail

Africa are not very different from those that other humans situated in other parts of the world have to deal with. The issues include but are by no means limited to the following: procuring a good living from the bounties of nature using the products of human ingenuity such as science and technology and by so doing freeing up more leisure for more people in which they can contemplate such arcane topics as the meaning of life, the best life for humans, what happens to us after we die, and ancillary themes. Put more specifically, Africans, no more or less than any other people, face the challenge of ensuring, for themselves and their posterity, lives that are free of the trinity of hunger, disease, and ignorance. They want to live in healthy environments. They want to lead hopeful lives where they can always expect that the future, near or far, will be better than the present, that they will have more control over the direction of their lives, that they will not live under regimes in the constitution of which they have had no hand, and that they will live long prosperous lives marked mostly by happiness.

I have said that all humans share the goals just adumbrated. But the goals assume some urgency in the African situation, given Africa's peculiar history. From about the sixteenth century until this writing, it hardly can be denied that Africa, most parts of it anyway, has not had the privilege of autochthony when it comes to the unfolding of socio-historical processes within it. First, it endured nearly three centuries of depredations brought on by the Trans-Atlantic Slave Trade. It transitioned from that into nearly a century of a colonialism that was quite unlike that anywhere else, which left the continent with a deliberate non-development of its productive forces—human and material—and made it essentially a vast rentier continent that supplies, in lieu of rent, the rest of the world, *sans* any value added, with raw materials that stoke the engines of commerce and manufacture in places far removed from Africa. People rightly expected and many Africans believed that the "wind of change" that ostensibly blew colonialism away from the continent would usher in "life more abundant" for their long-suffering population. No such thing happened. On the contrary, the continent passed under the twin evils of neocolonialism and military rule. It is not an exaggeration to say that Africa has yet to catch a break in almost half a millennium of its recent history.

Simultaneously, few will deny that Africa and its peoples deserve a break. I propose to argue in this manifesto that in order to join the forward march of the rest of the world—a world that has seen its erstwhile peers in misery in Asia and Latin America redeem the promise of "freedom for all, life more abundant" for their inhabitants—Africa must embrace, not just engage with modernity, and seek aggressively to install modern societies all across the continent. Put differently, I propose to do a spirited defence of the necessity of modernity as the way out of Africa's current prostrate position respecting the quality of life in it and the dismal prospects of its teeming majority.

This standpoint is informed in part by my realisation that the countries of Asia and Latin America that have transformed themselves for the better are precisely the ones that have wised up to the idea that—regardless of what they think of modernity and the West, which has benefited the most from its proliferation—a good way to improve their lot in the world is to borrow some pages from the West's playbook. I am not suggesting that they sought to become the West or that they uncritically appropriated Western forms and values. No, what they did was to realise that the concatenation of ideas and institutions represented in modernity held the most promise for the improvement of their lands and peoples. I am asking Africa, too, to do the same.

No doubt, the kind of polemic that I advance here is not new. There have been many essays and books that have called Africa on its failure to overcome its backwardness. The only difference is that many of such diatribes call for what are variously termed "African," "homegrown," or "indigenous" solutions to Africa's problems of hunger, disease, and ignorance. I eschew all such calls in what follows. I ask that Africa stop tiptoeing around modernity, stop its perfunctory engagement with it, expunge its ambivalence about it, and seek to realise the best that modernity has to offer for Africa's peoples.

I cannot be the only African who shares the point of view represented in this work. Part of why I have set out on this journey is that even though there must be many Africans who think that the continent should fully embrace modernity because it would be better off by doing so, there is a dearth of individuals making explicit cases for this attitude. This is not difficult to explain. The history of Africa's engagement with modernity has always been wracked with doubt, ambivalence, confusion, and hostility. Because the dominant thinking among Africans and non-Africans alike views modernity as coterminous with westernisation and because the West looms large in the making of the unhappy history of the continent recounted above, it is almost required of African scholars that they ritually reject anything Western or, at least, show that their relationship with it cannot be other than negative or ambivalent. I eschew any such ambivalence or hostility. The stakes are too high.

We need to distinguish between modernity and westernisation. The fact is that the two phenomena are separate and separable. Yes, the modernity that we place on offer in this work may have had its genesis, historically speaking, in Western Europe. Despite this genesis, it is inaccurate to suggest that its history was fully constituted there. Modernity may have originated in Western Europe but its history is not one with its European biography. Nor is it the case that all European countries share its heritage or that, when they do, they do so in the same way. Any credible history of modernity must reflect the global presence not just in its distribution but in its very constitution and that history cannot be complete if it omits the ways in which it has been modified in its motley migrations across the world's boundaries. In other words, how it has evolved over time has been determined by the history of interactions among Europeans, Africans, Asians, and Americans. And a true history of its discourse must reflect the many voices, traditions, and contestations that have shaped its evolution.

I am a careful student of this history. I refuse to yield to the triumphalists who wish to distort the real history of modernity and turn it into an ideological cudgel with which the West browbeats the rest of us into submission. In true modern spirit, I stake my claim to it and I wish to appropriate what is salubrious in it and use it as a salve on the spirit of a people who have been second to none in the construction of the material wealth of modernity and against whose humanity its ideological superstructure was fabricated. I wish to have Africa reclaim for itself and its peoples the benefits of modernity. This is the singular motivation for this manifesto.

Here a word of caution is in order. I do not advance modernity as the only or the absolute best form of social organisation possible for humanity. But it should be clear that I am not bothered by pedigree challenges. If you are an African and you are convinced that its Western provenance rules out modernity as a possible candidate for a solution to Africa's problems, or you are a so-called westerner who believes that the same provenance is proof of Africans' congenital inability to contribute anything to civilisation, I grant you your respective solitudes. All you need do is ignore this manifesto. If you are an African nativist who is of the belief that only "African" solutions will work, I wish you more power. But that is not the fish I wish to fry in this work. If on the other hand, you think that the path I am set on here is wrong-headed but are willing to engage the case it makes, I look forward to our exchange and mutual enrichment in divergence. This book may not change your mind, but I hope it, at least, forces you to rethink your initial orientation towards its claim.

Unfortunately, no thanks to the continuing conflation of westernisation and modernity and the unhappy history, on balance, of Africa's relations with the so-called West, a nationalist problematic that requires a ritual denunciation of the West, or no more than a muted admiration for it, makes for a difficult row to hoe for an enterprise such as the one embarked upon here. I shall pay no mind to the nationalist problematic. The nationalist problematic has done nothing except hold the continent back from progress. There is only one way for the nationalists to show their seriousness beyond mere talk: they should work to rid the continent of all significant traces of the modern legacy and strive toward the reinstallation of indigenous institutions, practices and processes with but the most minimal echoes of alien influences in them. It would not suffice for them to say that they would like to see modern institutions, practices, and processes adapted to African conditions. For if that is all they are asking for, there will be little or no difference between their goal and ours in this manifesto. And if they really mean it, then the attitude that they and pretty much most

African intellectuals have adopted towards modernity is at variance with what is called for by any serious desire to domesticate the phenomenon. To do the latter, one must avow a serious study of modernity's tenets, history, practices, institutions, and processes. I offer this discussion as a contribution to that avowal. To this end, I shall not only fail to denounce modernity in this work, I do not plan to say anything bad about it. Even though I distinguish between modernity and westernisation, I do not propose to say anything bad about the West either.

A kind of ritual throat clearing is almost mandatory in African discourse these days, and it is devoted to showing how the West cannot offer solutions to our problems and how the injection of western ideas into African culture is at the root of the continent's current predicament. I decline the offer to participate in this ritual. Why wouldn't I say anything bad about modernity or the West in this essay? The answer is simple. Africans, if the professions by their intellectuals are to be believed or, at the least, taken seriously, already know all that there is to know of all that is wrong with or bad about modernity and all its manifestations. And why wouldn't they know it. They live with it every day. In a world that increasingly mimics the "global village" foretold by Marshall McLuhan, they are too familiar in living colour and multimedia—radio, satellite TV, real time streaming video, etc.—with incidents of mass murder, serial killings, kids gone bad, child abuse, racism, and so on. They know too well that at the bottom of all these ills is the rapacious individualism of the West, read modern, which makes each the enemy of the rest, discourages fellow feeling and other regarding behaviour, provides easy recourse to violence, and, in sum, makes the Hobbesian state of nature an all too grim reality. In short, Africans are already suffused with knowledge of what is wrong with modernity and with the West, its prime embodiment.

Although Africans are adept at deciphering what is wrong with the West and with modernity, one must lament the fact that few bother to decipher what is right with either. Let us modify what we just said. Indeed, the irony is that Africans know what is right with modernity and with societies in which its principles reign supreme. We see evidence of this in the mad rush of African intellectuals as well as members of the middle and upper classes of African societies to avail themselves of the privileges and forbearances offered by modernity in the countries of not just the West but also Africa; here I have in mind the attraction of South Africa in recent times as a haven from the depredations of non-modern temperament in the rest of the continent. The evidence is irrefutable.

The African elite lead double lives. While they are busy trumpeting their nationalist credentials evidenced by their "staying home" and "building the nation"—doing very well for themselves, thank you—their lives are not complete unless they have easy passage to the countries of the West even if they have to buy that passage with their self-respect—personal and collective—and their national patrimony. They take their money—however they obtain it—and buy property or otherwise invest it in western countries and hope thereby to be able to come and go in those countries. Occasionally, they are roughened up by the customs and immigration officials of some of those countries. Nor are they ever free from the endemic racism of those same countries. The African elite are notorious for thundering against the inhumane treatments meted out to them by the functionaries of the countries in which they choose to invest their wealth, well- or ill-gotten. Protests are lodged with the diplomatic representatives of such countries accredited to their African homelands. Their local newspapers are full of expressions of indignation brimming with more than enough vituperation to sink the offending country, if words were water. Yet, I have never once heard an aggrieved African elite member forswear any more trips to those countries. And, more incredible still, no wealthy African—stolen or earned wealth, it does not matter—has ever announced divesting himself of his holding in the offending countries!

What is more, whenever there is a task that involves brain work—manifestations of the centrality of reason, about which we shall be saying more presently—the African elite, notoriously, turn to the West, especially its most modern members. African football authorities seem to think that a white skin is synonymous with superior coaching skills. How else does one explain their penchant for hiring lower grade coaches from Europe at scandalous rates of pay when better qualified Africans are expected to accept beggar remunerations in the name of some bastard patriotism? Or the penchant for seeking training locations in European countries when big campaigns are looming in international competitions?

Our parliamentarians would pay anything to be welcome to Westminster or Capitol Hill to be tutored by Britons and Americans in how to be parliamentarians. I suspect that they cannot wean themselves from the feeling that it adds to their "authenticity" if they could put on their resumés that they had attended "school" in the so-called West! Where do we look for models of institutions from schools to banks to even our common residences? The same West. We have kept the inherited languages of our colonisers because we are simply too lazy to develop our indigenous languages for twenty-first century tasks, including those of science and theoretical engagements. Such is our lack of self-respect that we end up hiring fourth-rate coaches and intellects—the ubiquitous "experts." Yet, we hate to be told to engage the best of what we care to borrow from the lands whence modernity originated.

The reason is not far to seek. Africans need access to Western countries as a fall-back position when things do not go well in their homelands—their love for which, they would like us to believe, is undying. I do not mean when they lose power or when they are on the run from the nationalism-inflected state when it turns on them. No, given the backward state of their countries, their lands cannot support their consumption patterns: shopping, entertainment, educating their children, or just plain "getting some fresh air." Given the muted freedom in their countries, many of them need the countries of the West for them to indulge in some of the excesses they cannot get away with in their homelands. Think of the homosexuals in their ranks. Think of the cross-dressers amongst them. This is why it is difficult for me to take them seriously when they rail against the West.

South Africa, the most modern country in Africa, has since 1994, offered a "Western" alternative closer to home. Many African scholars who would in the past have headed for the United States and other points west now scramble to go to South Africa. I have deliberately singled out for mention South Africa and not the southern African region for a very simple reason. Although quite a few have gone to Lesotho, Malawi, and Swaziland, South Africa and Botswana remain the preferred destinations. The reason, from the perspective that informs our manifesto, is simple. Apart from their strong economies, especially their currencies, Botswana also boasts, alongside Senegal, the longest surviving democratic polity in the continent. Meanwhile, since 1994, South Africa has realised the dream of the Freedom Charter, the dream of a multiracial, "rainbow nation" democracy which openly embraced many modern principles and is now actively seeking to realise them on the continent. Even as the nightmare of blacks was being intensified by the apartheid system, white South Africans managed to give themselves the most modern life in the continent. South Africa's rulers since 1994 have redeemed this legacy for all South Africans.

I am suggesting that Africans from outside South Africa do not gravitate towards the country because Ubuntu has taken up residence there or that the country is the paragon of African culture and traditions. These may all be true. But it is also true that South Africa has the most modern polity in the continent, without an iota of doubt. Its overwhelmingly liberal-inflected Constitution boasts more protection for heterodoxy than the United States' version. It does not shy away from the demands of the legal subject and its commitment to procedure—the hallmark of modern politico-legal systems—is without parallel in Africa. It is interesting that in the run-up to the adoption of their new constitution, South Africans were not belly-aching about how they were going to find and then enshrine some peculiarly African mode of governance that did not owe its inspiration to the evil West. Nor were they particularly willing to create pockets of so-called tradition in different parts of the country, a move that would have created a hierarchy of citizenships in South Africa.

Let us be very clear. There are elements of the South African order that pay attention to some of the values derived from the indigenous cultures in the country. But where its constitutional order is concerned, it is out-and-out modern. Its citizenship is singular, indivisible, and is effective over every inch of the geo-polity that is South Africa. When Zulu nationalists pressed for a special status for their nation within a free South Africa, their plea was rejected. I am yet to hear anyone speak of "nation-building" in South Africa. South Africa recognises its multinational character and provides for eleven official languages and does a fabulous job of selling the many cultural traditions it contains. It has many nationalities and cultural groups; but it has a singular citizenship and all who are admitted to it enjoy the same political and legal rights. That is why the world was disappointed and surprised when murderous xenophobic riots broke out in 2008 and it is why many South Africans apologised for and condemned the riots.

In case anyone still harbours any doubts as to the rootedness of the modern temper in South Africa, one need look no further than the resignation of Thabo Mbeki from the country's presidency on account of an allegation by a high court judge that his administration may have interfered with the independence of the judiciary. Although I believe that the forcible resignation extracted by his party, the African National Congress, violated due process, the fact that the issues were processed in terms of following rules and adhering to procedure is a specifically modern attribute. The fact that our nationalist friends find an alternative place to be really free in South Africa, minus the racist aggravations in western countries, counts in favour of our standpoint in this manifesto.

The example from South Africa is significant for its emulation of what is good in modernity to create a good life for its citizens. Here is a more perverse example of how Africans are not loath to copying from the West. The problem lies in what they consider is worth copying. Let us go to Ethiopia. The state-run television service in Ethiopia, in 2006, hosted its own version of the popular "Idol" programme that originated in Britain and has proliferated around the world. West Africa has also recently held its own version. But let us stick momentarily with Ethiopia. There they call it *Popular Idol*. As is often said, imitation is the best form of flattery. In seeking to replicate the *Idol* idea in Ethiopia, those who run the state TV service are acknowledging, even if they are wrong in their estimation, that there is something about the idea that makes it worthy of emulation. Ordinarily, one would celebrate the genius of any people who are not too proud to acknowledge a lack and are smart enough to fill it from across the border. So, in a sense, I do not want Ethiopians to give up on their version of the *Idol*. What I ask them to do is not to limit themselves to the frivolities of Western life and culture that the programme quintessentially embodies.

Part of why *American Idol* took off in the first place and is so successful is that the owners of the television media were willing to trust individuals, ordinary people at that, to come up with ideas that might translate to *American* or *British Idol*. Not only that, they could take a chance on a Simon Cowell and trust that the collective aversion to open criticism, even the occasional acerbic one, would not sound the death knell of the programme. Furthermore, they trust ordinary persons to judge and choose who they think deserves to be worshipped by them in the popular imagination! But enough of the *Popular Idol!*

It would have been very nice and, I daresay, much more rewarding for ordinary Ethiopians if their governors, who are so desirous of entertaining them, would also take their citizens' autonomy very seriously, recognise the right of their citizens to be the authors of their own life scripts and, most importantly, trust their ability to decide who rules over them in similar fashion to their electing whom to worship as their *Idol.* I would like them to look at an earlier borrowing in their history when the then Emperor, Haile Selassie I, looked to the Scottish legal system for a model for law reform. Maybe if he had taken seriously the most important aspects of that system, he would have evolved a genuine constitutional monarchy that would have assured respect for the dignity of Ethiopian citizens while preserving the cultural dominance of the throne. How nice would it be if the Ethiopian administration and those of other regions of Africa where the *Idol* has taken root would copy from the United Kingdom and the United States respect for the dignity of their citizens and seek to replicate the best of the Anglo-American legal system, especially its fastidious attachment to procedure and the right of the individual to be different for its own sake!

I provide one more example of how Africans know what is right with the West but reject avowing or deliberately seeking to emulate it. It is a cross between the profound and the jejune. May 1st is a day that is now almost universally celebrated as International Workers' Day. Needless to say, being almost universal, it is celebrated all across the African continent. In fact, I wrote this originally having just finished listening to reportage from the BBC Radio's "Focus on Africa" programme regarding the commemoration of the day from different parts of the continent, most notably Nigeria and Kenya. By itself, the celebration of May Day, as it is called, has become so routine in Africa that for one to suggest that the observance not be carried out will be a sure sign that she has lost her marbles. If any evidence be needed, one can find it in the ease, almost nonchalance, with which African workers, especially their leaders in the organised labour movement, sing "Solidarity forever," the international workers' anthem.

You, dear reader, may wonder why these commonplace activities deserve comment. Here is why. When I heard Kenyan trade unionists singing, even if poorly, "Solidarity forever," I wondered what this song really means for them. It is not unlikely that the same enthusiastic singers of this anthem who defend workers' dignity and its recognition and preservation, who berate governments and corporations alike for violating those rights, will strenuously demur were we to insist that they recognise, much less embrace, some of the related principles of social living traceable to the same tradition from which the inspiration for the holiday that they celebrate so ardently is derived: the West. This is not a trivial point. Indeed, as I have repeated *ad nauseam* in this discussion, part of why I have undertaken this project, what irks me, is not that African intellectuals—I number labour leaders among them—routinely play fast and loose with those parts of the Western heritage they wish to appropriate for Africa; they reserve the right to do so like any other people. What irks me is that we are forever skimming the surface of very complex realities—familiarisation with the histories of which might have saved African masses a whole lot of agonies.

For example, it is not an insignificant fact that the immediate impetus for the May Day observance occurred in Chicago, Illinois, in the context of labour, industry, and state relations in the United States. When the state brutally suppressed labour protests in 1886 and, in the aftermath, framed their leaders and incarcerated or executed them a year later, the self-same principles that I am urging upon my fellow Africans necessarily condemned that outcome and eventually secured pardons and belated recognition for those wrongly accused and punished. In dedicating itself to ensuring that that incident or others like it were never repeated, the American state, in spite of all its shortcomings that Africans seem to know better than its strengths, worked and continues to work to abridge the gap between what the United States aims to be and what it is at any given time. In so doing, it strives to reduce similar incidents. Can we say the same for our African celebrants of May Day? Do we take seriously the fundamental philosophical orientation that undergirds state-civil society relations in, say, the United States? I am arguing that if we were to do the latter, our continent would be a much better place to live for its inhabitants.

We love to emulate, and earnestly, too, the superficial aspects of modernity. I am sure that Nigerians own more digital television sets per capita than the inhabitants of South Korea, which not only manufactures them but is a world leader, via its Samsung and LG conglomerates, in research and development in flat screen digital technology. Kenyans have pioneered new uses for cell phones even though the country will not consider indigenising the science that provides the foundation for the operation of the devices. The continent will soon be awash in Tata Motors' Nano cars even though no African country thinks of research institutes that aim for the domestication of automotive technology. Where the consumption of technologies is concerned, Africa is a continent where anything goes. We are ultra-modern in all outward manifestations but our core is pre- and non-modern, and we do not seem to be agitated the least bit by this sad reality. That is why we would sing lustily the solidarity songs of the international labour movement; go to rallies all decked out in t-shirts and baseball caps, none of which frippery has indigenous origins.

There are numerous other ways in which the superficial aspects of modernity are more attractive to us.

And this is not on the score of these aspects being less onerous to accomplish than the more fundamental dimensions. One can cite here the popularity of various civil society groups that are an integral part of modernity's evolution and a mark, in Europe and North America, of its radical break with an aristocratic past dominated by ascription. The Rotary, Lions, Soroptimist, Circle K, and similar clubs are dedicated to charity, civic engagements, and mutual aid, including business networking activities. But they also challenge their members to show achievements that are emblematic of their claim to self-driven success. It is no accident that in their countries of origin, the leading lights of such clubs are often times successful professionals, solid members of the middle class, whose success owes to merit, not nature or birth. It is instructive that in their evolution, such clubs did not seek to encumber themselves with previous honorifics and the systems that legitimised them. No Lords, Counts, or Princes in their ranks or in their leadership. If there be any aristocracy, it is one of merit where recognition is bestowed on success in one's chosen career and success in one's contribution to civic life, the real domain of civil society and a peculiar emanation of the modern age.

Not only have we eagerly embraced the organisations, we have become, if only in numbers, their most enthusiastic wings. I remember when, in 1984, Nigeria had the second largest delegation, only smaller than that of the host country, at the world congress of Rotary International held in Toronto, Canada. But, I am sure, given our inability to count [about which see chapter 4 below], or to take counting seriously, not too many members of Nigeria's delegation thought for a single moment what a massive transfer of resources from Nigeria to Canada—airfare, hotel bills, boarding, shopping, etc.—their junket represented. Meanwhile, just as in other spheres, we have adopted the Rotarian shell, but not its animating spirit, its grounding philosophy, most notably, individualism. Yes, the Rotary club is emblematic of the modern relationship between the individual and the community. The individual is required to achieve but expected to turn around and give back to the community. This is not because the community was instrumental to the individual's success but because, as someone who has been blessed, he or she should oblige those who have been less circumstanced and, by so doing, add even more stature to herself. The Rotary club for us has become enmeshed in our ascriptive structures, headed by chiefs and chiefs-in-waiting, coveted more for the opportunities to travel and, most importantly, the networking privileges that attach to its membership.

We are not conflicted about embracing those things. Nor, as we showed above, are we conflicted about domesticating *Big Brother*, *The Apprentice*, *British Idol*, or *Who Wants to be a Millionaire?* and doing the best we can to mimic them right down to the wardrobe of the hosts and the programmes' scripts. When it comes to embracing the fundamental philosophical templates that made the societies which originated the programmes we love to copy such alluring models, we balk. It is then that we remember that the templates don't translate well into our environment. It is amazing that digital television technology translates very well even in the absence of regular power supply. In that case we are willing to subject our respiratory health to the fumes of generators imported to fit the template to our backward environment. When we have to confront the real causes of the superiority of those societies we suddenly become apostles of radical difference. We wish to protect Africa from the decadence of the West—a decadence we have no trouble replicating in the worst ways possible in the cyber cafes where our young now go to download and consume pornography or in the new XXX-rated clubs that are fast becoming a standard feature of our urban landscapes from Lagos to Nairobi. We love pornography but we would not change our archaic abortion laws to give our women control over their bodies and reduce, if not end, the carnage caused on a daily basis by the proliferation of back-room abortions in our countries.

The ideological template from which the institutions, practices, and processes are fashioned that we are all too eager to mortgage our self-respect and national patrimonies to enjoy in modern countries, does not receive the appropriate level of attention that it deserves nor the serious engagement with and embrace that redeeming the promise of a good life for our masses requires. We spend millions on the self-help books that are coming out of Euro-America and are busy replicating them in our homelands. But it never occurs to us to ex-plore the notion of the self that is at the base of all such discourse. We love to deceive ourselves.

Our capacity for and evidence of self-deception on a mass scale regarding our relationship to modernity and its associated principles, practices and processes is what has made me challenge us to come out and wrestle modernity's beast directly without ifs, buts, or other ali-bis. If you are inclined to reject modernity, this book aims to make it easier for you to do so: you will at least have a better grounding in the concatenation of ideas that you are rejecting. If, on the other hand, like me, you wish to embrace modernity, this book should enhance your un-derstanding of the object of your admiration and move you to think up ways of installing its principles in ways that redeem its promise for Africans even as it is inte-grated into their historical experience.

I have written this book primarily to speak for that party to which Africans like me belong, who be-lieve that a serious embrace of modernity moderated, of course, by our historical experience is the best way to move the continent forward at the present time. Hence, I call it a manifesto. To those who might be inclined to think either that there is no such party or that its mem-bers must be so few as to be inconsequential, I would like to say that they are mistaken in their belief. There are many reasons for the relative absence of this viewpoint in public discourse and scholarship in and about Africa.

Many members of this party have been intimidated into silence by the overwhelming transaction costs of appearing to canvass anything "western" in the African public space. Anyone who departs, or calls on others to depart, from the dominant orientation that Africans are by nature communalistic and African culture has developed in the main along communalist trajectories is marked for ridicule, abuse, and hostility. Even if we grant the truth of these affirmations, we must qualify it. Unless we wish to say that African societies do not grow and human nature does not evolve in Africa, we must affirm that Africans and their social forms are not unlike their other numbers in the rest of the world. Insofar as this is the case, it stands to reason that they, too, must be evolving: Africans, too, are historical peoples. This means that even if we wish to affirm continuities in their history, we must not do so in complete obliviousness of the many and diverse influences that have impacted those histories. Given the severity of the impact of some of those historical movements, it stands to reason that the communalism of African traditions must have undergone severe disruptions such that what is obtained now of those traditions cannot but be marked. There is a need for serious updating. Unfortunately, much of the discourse on African communalism is afflicted with a terminal case of ahistoricity and its defence usually unfolds as if the same simple societies are the ones for which contemporary social theory should be designed.

Simultaneously, because of the unhappy history of our relations with the West, African scholars are, on pain of name-calling, dismissal as inauthentic, and stig-matisation as self-haters, frightened off any canvassing of things western. We who believe that Africans should exercise the basic prerogative of all humans to borrow, as they deem fit, from their fellow humans across his-torical and cultural boundaries whatever ideas, practices, processes, principles, and institutions the adaptation of which to their context would help improve their societies on the road to creating the most conducive conditions for human efflorescence, and should refuse to be intimidated. I hope that this manifesto gives voice to more members of our party to speak up, out, and loud on behalf of the rel-evance of modernity to moving Africa to a better future.

Another reason why the members of the modern party have not been as forthcoming as we should be is that there is also a lot of ambivalence in our ranks that to be modern is to be western and any attempt on our part to fly modernity's banner will be mistakenly construed as a continuation of our subordination to European coun-tries and prototypes. This fear is misplaced but its roots are easy to trace. Those of us who wish to see a mod-ern transformation in Africa are not well grounded in its fundamental tenets and enabling philosophical presup-positions. In other words, education in the discourse of modernity is limited and, in many cases, relatively unso-phisticated. The result is that many of us canvass various tenets of modernity without evincing any consciousness that that is what we are doing. It is part of the object of this manifesto to enable us to nod in assent to and adopt every philosophical idea expounded in what follows that enables us to make better sense of insights we already possess and illuminate stances we have previously taken. It should make us more willing to study the idea and better able to justify our preference.

We should be able to advance modernity as an idea and movement with some unity in spite of the multiple voices that have shaped it over time. I have isolated what I consider to be some of the core ideas associated with modernity, and by showing how Africa has been remiss in not taking those ideas seriously and how the continent stands to be prospered by their embrace, I expect that my readers will garner more illumination than if I had offered a philosophical discourse. For illustration, from a discussion of the philosophical ground of the individualism that typifies modernity—the principle of subjectivity—we find that an individual who is not the author of her life script would be a defective being. The same goes for groups that are constituted by adherents of modernity. While they hew strictly to the broad philosophical principles of modernity, each society will adapt the movement in accord with its history. This should put to rest all anxieties about how to be modern is to be like the West. Personally, I do not have any problem with being like the West. After all, I, too, am a westerner! But this is not the place to expound the grounds for this claim. Taking seriously some of the paths cleared in the following chapters is sure to enable more of us to work our way to and through the labyrinths of modernity.

Two

The Sticky Problem of Individualism

Why are Africans hostile to individualism, the dominant principle of social ordering and living under modernity? There are diverse possible answers but, in light of our primary focus on modernity, a case can be made for the fact that much of the hostility directed at individualism originates from the conflicted legacy of modernity and colonialism in the continent.

I WOULD like to begin by offering a variation on a Yorùbá proverb: "If you wish to see the red of an African intellectual's eye, that is, draw the ire, especially of an academic, merely suggest that the continent and its peoples come to grips with the idea of individualism and all that it entails." One can only imagine what might follow a suggestion that Africans embrace individualism as a principle of social ordering. What this means is that for African intellectuals, individualism and all that it entails are fighting words, the utterance of which is likely to be followed by testiness, frostiness, hostility, sometimes abuse and, in the worst of cases, verbal violence. Yet, I would like to insist in this chapter that it is way past time that Africans, especially their intellectuals, engaged with and embraced, yes, embraced individualism and some of its manifestations. This looks simple enough. Yet, it is almost impossible to have any decent debate about this among Africans.

Again, I cannot, and I am not inclined, to claim that I would be the first African scholar to canvass a deep understanding of or engagement with individualism. I doubt, though, that there have been too many advocates for the sort of stand taken in this section. I would like to argue that the long-standing opposition to individualism and to most of its ramifications in the African imaginary must abate if Africa is to move forward with the rest of the world.

Why are Africans hostile to individualism, the dominant principle of social ordering and living under modernity? There are diverse possible answers but, in light of our primary focus on modernity, a case can be made for the fact that much of the hostility directed at individualism originates from the conflicted legacy of modernity and colonialism in the continent. African scholars love to tell stories of African communalism, of how Africans are communalistic almost by nature, and how, beginning in the nineteenth century, what they have identified as "the African personality" is so different from other personalities in the rest of the world that they consider the assault on and near destruction of it under the combined onslaught of first Christianity and later colonialism as one of the signal losses suffered by the continent and its peoples under those alien historical movements.

This is how the narrative goes. Before the irruption of Christianity and colonialism into their land and mindscapes, communalism was the dominant and preferred mode of social living and principle of social ordering in much, if not all, of Africa. It is very difficult to locate clear and concise definitions of communalism in much of the writing about the idea. For our purposes, a rough characterisation should suffice. Communalism, in the present context, is the view that a people prefer to and predominantly live in community. Since this is not a peculiarity of any people but almost a defining feature of our basic humanity, it must be the case that communalism is intended to mean more than the commonplace we just stated. On this score, communalism is a mode of social living in which living together, communal living, is to be preferred. As well, it is a principle of social ordering under which, in the relationship between the individual and the community, the community is held superior to the individual, and where their interests come into conflict, those of the community should prevail. And it should not be forbidden to bend the will of the individual or sometimes abridge his or her interests if doing so would serve the ends of the community. In such a setting, the community and its interests are supreme, and it suffices to cite such interests to justify interfering with individual preferences even in those areas that relate to how an individual wants to be in the world and what he or she takes to be the good life and the means for attaining it.

It is said that the individual was not only recognised but was also accommodated and her interests and well-being were well protected and taken care of. We must not make light of this contention. Each one was her fellow's keeper. Strangers were welcomed and provided with victuals and a place to lay their heads. Mothers took care of children. Actually, strictly speaking, what I just said is incorrect. The rearing of children was not tied to the matter of who bore them. Everyone, or at least every adult in the neighbourhood, took responsibility for the rearing of children in their vicinity, regardless of who bore them. Young mothers were not left alone to take care of themselves and their infant children. Wives took care of their husbands and their families; husbands did the same for their wives and the latter's families. Building houses, clearing land, planting and harvesting crops were never the sole responsibility of any single individual. Each went to help others execute such tasks, and they in turn were there for each other when each individual's own time came for help. In short, it is hard to argue that anyone would be left untaken care of in a context in which everyone was required to look out for and take care of other people in the community.

You are right to wonder, dear reader, where is the individual in all this? Of course, and this is the crux of communalism as a principle of social ordering, the individual is somewhere there in the mix. It is just that she is lost in the collective thicket. She is palpably inferior to the collective and few were those circumstances in which her interest or preference or say-so would trump those of the group or community. It is almost as if there is a pact between the individual and the community under which, in return for being taken care of by everyone else, the individual forgoes any significant exercise of will in the ordering of his life. In other words, the individual is accommodated insofar as he is willing to be subsumed in the embrace of the group. Meanwhile, all the other attributes of the individual remained intact: individual names, mine and thine, heroism, and so on. But, when all is said and done, the community rules and that's that.

If Africans are to be believed, the arrangement worked quite well. Great nations rose and fell as in other areas of the world; people lived well and their communities prospered. There was very little, if any, destitution because when there was abundance it was shared, and when there was scarcity, it was shared as well. Everyone pulled for the success and prosperity of their communities. This pretty much is the story that Africans love to tell of their forebears before the killjoy foreigners came and put paid to the good old days.

Before we go on to consider in detail the new mode of social living and its attendant principle of social ordering that shook the African world out of its orbit, I would like to suggest that, no matter one's preference, the story that we have been considering sounds too good to be true. Indeed, it is easy to see that it could only have been true of the simplest of societies marked by small size, undifferentiated populations and unanimity of opinions. That is, in the name of underscoring how different Africans and their culture are from the rest of common humanity, African scholars actually end up providing needless fodder for the cannons of anti-African racism. How do they do this? It is a fundamental pylon of racial supremacist discourse that Africans and their descendants in different parts of the world are either not a part of the human race or are so different from other humans that they are considered barely human. Every time African scholars and their overseas sponsors or sympathisers play what we call the "difference game" they reinforce this racist mentality. It is time to get rid of this game.

Once we get past the game and its surrogates, we find that there is no human society that, at a time closest to its inception, was not communalistic in its mode of social living. But any society with any degree of complexity would have begun to distance itself from the undifferentiated totality once it evolved a distinction between mine and thine. Does this mean that individualism immediately supplanted communalism as a mode of social living? By no means. The emergence of more advanced forms of social differentiation beyond that of mine and thine meant that even when communalism remained the dominant mode of social living, it did not remain the only principle of social ordering.

This is not the place to cash out the philosophical niceties suggested by these distinctions. What is of moment here is that in societies marked by high levels of social differentiation sometimes manifested in hierarchies marked by superordinate/subordinate relationships, it rings less true to speak only of horizontal relations marked by mutual concern and coordinate or complementary status. In such situations, we must expect some relationships characterised by inequality, marked by exploitation of some by others, whereby many produced surplus enough to enable some to live without having to work, and so on. If indeed Africans built complex civilisations that included sophisticated systems of governance, socio-economic division of labour, not to talk of complicated ideological structures, it stands to reason that even if they retained communalism as their principal mode of social living and dominant principle of social ordering, they must have embodied significant heterodoxy and difference among their diverse populations.

Hence, we must expect that in spite of all the good that is attributed to communalism over time, there must have been a minority of individuals who didn't care much for the play of community and its overwhelming influence in their lives. That is, we can imagine that in those days of yore there were Africans who were contrarians, who sought to do things differently, who did not think that the ways of the community were the only or even the best ways of doing things, who desired to have a social arrangement that was more accommodating of individual preferences, and who could not wait to jump at the opportunities for these alternative ways of being human when first Islam and then the second wave of Christianity came ashore in their communities.

Certainly, the history of Christianity in Africa goes back to the very inception of the faith itself. But on the coast of West Africa and the rest of the continent outside of North and Northeast Africa, the introduction of Christianity followed different trajectories. The first wave of Christianity landed on the West and Southwest coast in the fifteenth century and fizzled out after a while. At that time, too, the missionaries tried to take advantage of the then communalism of African societies by converting African rulers in the hope that where the leaders led the rest would follow. It is a testimony to the resident heterodoxy in those societies that the project failed in all the places where it was tried.

Then came the nineteenth century and, in the aftermath of the abolition of Slavery and the Trans-Atlantic Slave Trade, a new wave of missionaries landed on the west coast of Africa. There were some fundamental differences between this latter movement and the former one described above. In the first place, the new Christianity is a post-Reformation variant which meant that instead of the previous Catholic version characterised by monopoly, there was a variety of protestant denominations competing for the souls of the African natives. Secondly, as a result of development during the Trans-Atlantic Slave Trade and the evolution of New World Slavery as well as the activities of the Humanitarian and Aboli-

tionist Movement, there was a veritable African component in the new cohort of missionaries desirous of fishing
for native souls. That is, a good part of the evangelisation
undertaken from the nineteenth century on was driven
by native agency which may, in part, explain its widespread and stupendous success.

Finally, this new variant of Christianity formed
a good part of the genesis of, and in fact was barely distinguishable from, a larger movement: modernity. By
that time, the modern age had come into its own and the
basic tenets of modernity would become the ideological
template for social transformation that the new evangelisation brought in its wake. These three characteristics
are: (1) the principle of subjectivity; (2) the centrality of
reason; and (3) the idea of progress. They combined to
herald a new reality shaped by modernity and which, we
argue, was stymied when colonialism was imposed on the
continent beginning in the latter half of the nineteenth
century.

One of the core tenets of modernity is the preference for individualism as a mode of social living as well as
a principle of social ordering. It is this individualism that
is at issue in the present discussion. This is the individualism that constitutes a sticky problem in African discourses, theories, and social practices. The mentioning of
this idea is the equivalent of fighting words in discussions
with African scholars. Although hostility is rife among
Africans towards the ideas associated with individualism,
there is little evidence that African scholars and sundry

intellectuals have ever cared to unpack what these ideas entail and what might be good about them.

As is the case throughout this work, it is my contention that Africa would do very well indeed, first, if its peoples were to familiarise themselves with the idea of individualism and, second, embrace it in some measure as both a mode of social living and a principle of social ordering. Again, consonant with the general tenor of this manifesto, I take it that Africans do not need me to educate them on the ills and evils that attend individualism: they know them too well already and this knowledge explains their unease with and hostility towards it. Africans already know that under a mode of social living characterised by individualism, individuals are ravaged by loneliness, mutual hostility, lack of other-regarding concern, excessive pursuit of individual fulfilment even at the expense of the community and, in the twilight of their lives, such individuals are herded into old people's homes where they are at the mercy of stranger caretakers who abuse them or, at a minimum, fail to extend to them the kind of loving tenderness that would have been theirs in a communalist-oriented social setting.

What is more, where individualism is the principle of social ordering, in the Africans' understanding of it, the individual is prior and superior to the community and the interests of the community are routinely sacrificed to those of the individual. Where there is a conflict between the individual and the community, the individual often wins; the community is not permitted to bend

the will of the individual to conform to communal preferences and the individual in her person, place, or plan of
life may not be interfered with except at the invitation of
the individual concerned.

Just as in the case of the communalist story, the
story that Africans tell themselves of individualism, too,
is somewhat off the mark. But let us even assume that
the story is partly true—and I concede that it is—it does
not in any way encompass the whole of individualism
as both a mode of social living and a principle of social
ordering. Here I would like to offer my fellow Africans
an account of individualism as a core tenet of modernity
that endeavours to present it in positive light and shows
how Africa, as part of a positive critical engagement with
modernity, will be prospered.

The modern idea of individualism, understood as
a mode of social living, is built on a philosophy of separation. Communalism is founded on the affirmation of an
organic connection among those who make up a human
community. In the view of some African communalists
such is the nature of this connection that to be an individual, a person, requires that one be connected with the
community. Absent it, one is a nonentity. In the modern
conception, on the contrary, individuals are fundamen-
tally separated from one another. What is more, these
separated individuals come to the world as persons who,
to that extent, are not needful of other individuals for
being what they are: persons. Of course, they live in communities and their social living is made up of relations

among individuals that are no different from those that mark communalist societies. The critical difference is that whereas in the latter those relations are adjudged necessary, in modern individualism, they are considered contingent, products of negotiations—hence, the dominance of the idea of contract—among and between individuals. The underlying assumption here is that even though individuals may and do cooperate with one another, such cooperation is not essential to their personhood in both its constitution and its action in the world. Certainly, the individual needs others. But it satisfies this need based on its calculation of its interests and how best to attain or advance them. This is a fundamental difference between modernity-inflected individualism and other types of individualism.

There is an irony here that deserves some airing. Precisely because there is no entitlement in the relationship that individuals have with one another in an individualist setting, each knows that she must cultivate the other if they are going to have a mutually rewarding relationship. The upshot is that the problem of free riding is pushed to the surface and seriously and continually addressed in both theory and practice. In theory at least, each always considers the impact of his actions on his fellows. Of course, we have enough incidence of self-preferential behaviour in such societies. The difference is that no one thinks that another owes her anything that is not a product of their mutual consideration of what such behaviour will add to their respective self-interests.

In communalist society, on the other hand, as individuals, we take one another for granted. Because many of us have been socialised into thinking that individuals don't matter or, when they do, this must not be openly acknowledged or solicited, we end up not cultivating one another as we should. Family members think that their successful members owe them something for the sheer fact of their being members of the same family. Damn the family member who withholds help to another member on account of the latter not having earned the former's consideration in the sharing of his fortune. We take advantage of each other, and we dare not complain when we are victims!

It is not only in its account of the nature of the relationships between and among individuals, and those between individuals and the groups to which they belong or in which they participate, that this individualism differs from its other versions. The individual who is not organically connected to any other is for this reason adjudged free. In fact, it is a basic claim that the modern individual is a free being whose nature is typified by freedom. He is free to be whatever he wishes to be as long as he does not in the process impair the ability of others to similarly display or exercise their freedom. This means that we may not force another to our point of view, even when, especially when, it is within our power to do so whether as individuals or as groups. That is, we are enjoined to let the individual be—in all his utter difference from or with what we might prefer as an identity, a way of life, and so on. This emanates from that attribute of the modern individual that is at the core of that philosophical orientation: autonomy.

Thanks to this attribute, we are disabled from telling the individual how to lead her life, what to do with it, even when it is obvious that the choices being made by the individual concerned are unlikely to enhance her welfare. Yes, we may counsel and remonstrate with her, do our best to persuade her that her choices are injurious to her interests as we understand them from relating with her. But she is the ultimate judge of what to do with our advice; whether or not to accept it. We must never deign to be the best judge of what is good for any individual other than ourselves. We shall be examining momentarily some implications of what we have so far described as the individualist mode of social living.

We do not respect individuals because we love their choices or agree with them or even find them agreeable in the least. Indeed, we are required to respect them more so when we hate their choices and are repulsed by who they are or what they do. Respecting them for their sheer membership of the human species is what marks the modern age. Of course, I'd be reminded by many of the fact that there is nothing special about the modern requirement for respect for the humanity of every individual. Critics will be quick to point out that all the religious traditions insist that the dignity of each individual be recognised, affirmed, and respected. However, I would like to rejoin by reminding my critics of the fact that this widespread concern with respect for the individual in all these traditions did not preclude their denigration of women and repeated diminution of their worth; the treatment of children in some as "property" or appendages of their parents, especially their fathers and the extending to such fathers of the privilege of doing as they wish with their progeny; the occurrence of human sacrifice in others; the enslavement of some by others in the name of the self-same religion; and the list goes on. All religions have in some way or the other, at one time or the other, been guilty of some of the defects just stated.

Yes, modernity and its philosophers condoned, make that justified, slavery and the dehumanisation of Africans as well as the extermination of Jews and other groups in its history. That is, I am sure to be reminded of the fact that the modern age gave us Slavery and the Atlantic Slave Trade, colonialism, and the Holocaust. No doubt, this was true. But we need to remind our critics, too, that it was in the name of the self-same modern principles that people fought back and prevailed over those horrors. When African Americans created civil rights jurisprudence in the United States, it was not done in the name of a demand for a new founding document for the polity. They merely insisted that the defenders of "western civilisation" stop lying to themselves and others, take seriously and implement faithfully the dictates of their creed, specifically as it was inscribed in the United States constitution.

It is worthy of note that modern states like the United States and the United Kingdom have had segments of their population apologise for the slave trade and slavery. Various Christian denominations have taken responsibility for their complicity in various acts of inhumanity in the past. Arabs have never apologised for enslaving Africans. Islam has not issued any *mea culpa* for the Trans-Saharan Slave Trade. Much of the human rights discourse at the present time has its birth certificate in the politico-philosophical discourse of modernity. A handful of African leaders and groups, too, have apologised for the complicity of their forebears in the iniquitous traffic in human beings that the slave trade was. One does not have to be an apologist for the West to grant that modernity, precisely for its contradictions, has a better record of correcting itself and appearing to make amends for some of its excesses.

The current open warfare on gays and lesbians across the African continent does not inspire confidence in our ability and willingness to take the individual and the heterodoxy that is bound to it seriously. In 2009, the Nigerian parliament introduced a bill to criminalise same-sex marriage. This represented a severe escalation of the ongoing warfare on gay and lesbian Nigerians. It got worse in Uganda where a bill was drafted that would have made having homosexual relations a capital offence conviction for which would have attracted the death penalty. It was not until Uganda was confronted with the real prospect of losing its foreign aid—so much for national independence and pride—especially from the United States, that the rulers of the country pretended that they had given up the folly. We know that that is not the case. The presidents of Zimbabwe and Namibia routinely whip up anti-homosexual sentiments against their gay citizens. Lesbians have been raped in South Africa in the crazy belief by their attackers that such assault would cure the women concerned of their homosexuality. And in Malawi, in 2010, two men were sentenced to 14-year jail terms with hard labour for seeking to affirm in marriage their love for each other! Yes, they were pardoned by the president of the country. The point, though, is that human rights should not be contingent on the kindly disposition of a country's rulers however benevolent they may be.

What I have found disheartening about these sordid episodes is that few human rights groups have come out boldly in support of the right of our gay and lesbian citizens to live and enjoy their sexual preferences. It was left to a group of gays in Nigeria, organised in what they call the Queer Alliance, to rally against this assault on the human rights of a group of citizens. Even more disheartening, to take just one example, has been the reaction of some of Nigeria's newspaper columnists and academics who, in columns and op-ed pieces in some of the country's major newspapers, have railed against homosexuality and same-sex marriage. As well, an ex-president of Nigeria insisted that homosexuality just isn't right in light of his Christian beliefs. The bases for their opposition include, according to them, the fact that homosexuality is forbidden by God; it is an import from the decadent West which has no place in Africa; it is forbidden by African culture. As some of them put it, if God had wanted same-sex marriage, he would not have created Adam and Eve as our progenitors.

There are so many things wrong with these justifications that I hardly know where to begin. In the first place, I am astounded at the illiteracy of the newspaper columnists regarding the history of human rights and the fact that rights are not culture bound. Nor are they to be embraced as suits our immediate preferences. The irony is lost on our eminent columnists that there is some incongruity in their defence of a right to freedom of expression and their repudiation of the right of homosexuals to lead their lives as they deem fit, as long as those who participate in it do so of their own will. In fact, both rights have the same root: the fundamental nature of humans as free beings. When they thundered that we cannot have freedom without limits, they betrayed their fundamental ignorance of the philosophical grounds of the idea of freedom in the modern era that we discussed above.

Their mishmash of Christian fundamentalism and African cultural fundamentalism is even more laughable. The Christianity that they now use to hide their homophobia and the founding myth of which they now use to legitimise hatred towards gay and lesbian citizens is also a western inheritance. Even our priests, especially the Anglican Church in Africa—which, given its origins in protest, ought to know better—and other religious functionaries are not exempt from partaking of this sad feast of hatred and duplicitousness. The irony is lost on them that it was originally in the name of that same Christianity that they are so enthusiastic to deploy as a cudgel against those with whom they disagree now that their forebears were enslaved and turned into chattel in the Americas; that their forebears were forbidden to marry white people on the pain of death or incarceration; that their forebears were violated, maimed in motley ways, and made to view their indigenous cultural inheritance with disdain and loathing. This is yet another way in which we cherry pick what to embrace of modernity. I sometimes wonder: is the story of Adam and Eve African?

Meanwhile, the same West that perpetrated the crimes just iterated has come to see the errancy of its ways and has been trying in its countries to move its humanity to a better place ever since. It has repudiated the ideologies that it used to imperialise and inflict violence on millions in various parts of the world. This includes, crucially, the recognition of the radical individuality of each of God's children and their right to be who they are; including being gays and lesbians if that is how they have turned out. I wonder why they stop short of embracing the progress that the West has made in recognising the humanity of their gay and lesbian compatriots and accommodating same in their social and political arrangements. What is most embarrassing about our column-ists' and leaders' condemnation of homosexuality is their presumption, based on an empty arrogance, that they already know the truth about morality and can, there-fore, lay down the law for their cohort. Part of the legacy of modernity is a plea for some humility and skepticism where matters of morals and ethics are concerned. We shall have more to say about this throughout this work.

The growing movement in a country like Nigeria and the widespread tendency in other countries, espe-cially in Islamic societies, to curtail, especially in, of all places, universities, modes of self-expression, particularly in dressing, is cause for pause amidst claims of respect for human rights and the dignity of the person. It seems as if we collectively think that once we put up a show, even a strong show at that, of defending what are generally termed human and civil rights, we have discharged the responsibility of taking the individual seriously. The fact that I am writing this is proof that I do not think that the responsibility is that easily dismissed or discharged.

Certainly, there are human rights groups in the continent. And one should not belittle the achievements of such groups over the years especially in the restoration and expansion of democratic rule in the last two dec-ades. I also recognise the work that those groups con-tinue to do in the continent regarding the safeguarding of human rights for groups and individuals in various countries even as it becomes clear that many so-called democratic regimes in Africa are so in name only. Witness the proliferation of human and civil rights lawyers across the continent and many among their ranks have made their careers peddling their credentials as defenders of human rights and the like. What bothers me is that such advocates, given their numbers and their otherwise loud protestations in other situations, have not been as loud or as insistent when it comes to the rights of homosexuals in various African countries. Not only are they relatively silent, I have no doubt that if we were to poll some of them, they would, like the Nigerian examples we discussed earlier, readily concede their own personal opposition to homosexuality on grounds ranging from its unnaturalness to its unafricanness to its sheer inhumanness. This is where I come in.

I was once at an academic conference in an African country where a leading official of the learned society that organised the conference vehemently condemned the South African constitutional order for being more liberal than that of the United States and, specifically, for protecting the rights of homosexuals in South Africa, including their right to contract marriages. The academic decried the South African constitution as another example of Africa being trampled by the jackboots of western imperialism. Fortunately, I was not the only one present who was offended by the comments. But I have mentioned it because just as in the case of the human and civil rights activists, few among us who were disgusted by our colleague's comments are likely to come out and openly canvass the rights of homosexuals in our various communities.

Lest I be misunderstood, my defence of the right of homosexuals to be does not owe anything whatsoever to my view of the rightness or wrongness, desirability or undesirability, of homosexuality and the behavioural consequences that it entails. Homosexuality or whatever else we care to focus on, where human conceptions of the good life and how to attain them are concerned, wherever no harm is intended or done to another and the exercise of one's choices does not preempt the exercise of the same by one's cohort, no basis exists for criminalising the choice concerned or even placing prohibitive transaction costs on it. In other words, what matters where protecting the rights of the individual is concerned is not whether or not the individual's behaviour attracts our approbation; rather what matters is that we respect that individual's rights to have, hold, and seek to realise her conception of the good life and the means to actualise it. This is a modern inheritance, and we are right to adjudge a society as modern or not by how well it seeks to make this one of the fundamental principles of social living within its borders.

African human rights activists should stop hiding under the idea of the culture-bound nature of rights or claiming some special African inflection for the rights of the individual in the modern dispensation. There is nothing peculiar about the African situation beyond the ugly fact that homophobia is not only condoned, it is respectable and, worse, in some states it is policy. Just looking at the United States and the unfortunate alliance between many in the African American community, especially the black clergy, and the hatred-spewing denizens of the so-called right wing, we see that intolerance is not, in this case, culture-bound. Only the language in which hatred is expressed differs. We cannot allow this unfortunate trend to continue. There is a lot riding on how we manage the condition of the most vulnerable among us.

Individualism is also a principle of social ordering. Remember that in the case of communalism the group or community is prior and superior to the individual and that the individual should always or in most cases be subordinate to and, from time to time, have her will bent to the interests and welfare of the community. Under individualism, construed as a principle of social ordering, the individual is sovereign. The idea of the sovereignty of the individual is central to the organisation of the modern state especially respecting its relation to the individuals whose activities it directs, moderates, and, on occasion, punishes; the idea of citizenship undergirds the privileges and forbearances that attach to the private lives of individuals in the modern state; the pattern of relations among the citizens; and generally sets the limits of what one may or may not do to, on, around or with the body and associated properties of another.

In a community in which the sovereignty of the individual predominates, when the free individual says no to an idea, action, or programme designed to advance the good of the community, we may not proceed to compel her to fall into line. The freedom of the individual in its modern inflection is ultimately summed up in the right to be different, "to be let alone," all for no other reason or goal than its own sake. Freedom is the quintessential mode of being human. Freedom here is, in this acceptation, presumably without limits. This is an important qualification. Certainly, there are limits imposed by our mortality, by the fragility of our physical constitution, and the general features that we share with all organic nature. Beyond that, there are limits imposed by the requirement that each individual's freedom be coextensive with an equal amount of freedom for his fellows. This is necessary because the formal equality of all necessitates that no one have more freedom than is available to her fellows.

With this description of limits it is easy to think that every time we think freedom we should do so with its limits. That would be mistaken. In its basic meaning, we think of freedom in terms of leaving the individual free to move in the world; we do not think of limiting the individual's room to manoeuvre. Rather, we invoke the implicit limits when the acting individual shows by the evidence of his action that he has acted in such a way as to diminish the equal freedom of his companions. One such way is when he has so acted as to injure or otherwise impair the ability of another to act in and on the world. That is what is meant when we say that freedom has no limits.

That is why, in countries where they take seriously the idea of freedom at work in this discussion, their constitutions do not contain the clawback clauses that African constitutions are notorious for. Clawback clauses are those ubiquitous clauses in African constitutions which give and take away in one and the same breath the rights of individuals. They go something like the following: every person is entitled to freedom of conscience, except when it shall be in the interest of state security to restrict or revoke it. Constitutional provisions regarding human rights should be stated in their unboundedness, the inherent limits left to be articulated by the courts when they are alleged to have been contravened. In other words, there should be no prospective limits that have the effect of preempting action and, in so doing, constrict rather than expand the sphere available for individuals to realise their life plans.

Of course, there are times when we may compel an individual to act against his or her will. As long as she is deemed to be a signatory to the social contract on which the society or community is based—an outcome based on the individual's capacity to partake in the constitution of the government that seeks to compel her expressed in the instrumentality of the franchise—she may be compelled to discharge her civic responsibility. Even then, this power to compel performance is never absolute; yet another marker of the salience of the individual over the group. The individual may insist on being exempted on the ground that performance conflicts with the dictates of her conscience; yes, the dictates of her conscience. There are fewer indices of the sovereignty of the individual than this recognition and deployment of the right to freedom of conscience.

The individual is supposed to be the author and owner of her beliefs or lack thereof. When she shares her beliefs with others she is supposed to have her own reasons for holding them. This is so because, ultimately, she is the one who would be held responsible for those beliefs and the consequences of any action that may proceed from them. Furthermore, as a possessor of reason, the individual is required to subject everything, especially beliefs, to the light of reason and embrace only those that survive reason's harsh and unforgiving searchlight. Appeals to authority, tradition, or revelation, are not forbidden but they are all inferior to reason's judgment. Given this foundation, it is no surprise that once we are persuaded that the individual has proceeded along rational lines in settling upon her beliefs, and they happen not to converge with those of the majority, or the most salient segments of the society, we are bound to respect her right to be different. That's it: the right to be different!

At the base of this right to be different in matters of beliefs, including morals, religious faith, sexual preference, and how to conduct one's private life, is a basic recognition that is another part of the modern inheritance: the fallibility of our judgment arising from the radical insufficiency of our cognitive tools. It informs the dominant skepticism about morals that marks modern societies and it requires that no one presume to have a lien on the truth that is otherwise unavailable to his compeers. Because we cannot be sure that we have happened upon the right or the good, given our fallibility, it behooves us not to outlaw another's departure from orthodoxy. It is why the freedom of conscience is so integral to the modern arrangement and why it is wrong to force another to conform to a view or an arrangement that, she is persuaded, may not be right.

When leaders, government functionaries, intellectuals, and other moulders of public opinion proclaim with certitude the wrongness or immorality of certain conceptions of the good life they happen to disagree with, they arrogate to themselves a cognitive competence that, in the modern dispensation, is available to no human. What is more, when a leader of the Anglican Church makes similar proclamations, he commits the same overreach. After all, infallibility has never been one of the doctrinal attributes of the Primate of the Anglican Church of Nigeria or of the Archbishop of Canterbury.

The basic freedom of the individual undergirds the attitude to that peculiar phenomenon of the modern age: the conscientious objector. It is thanks to the commitment to the right to freedom of conscience that the status of a conscientious objector commands recognition and forbearance. It is amazing how, in the modern state, the monopoly of arms and the plethora of politico-legal structures under the control of its directors are peremptorily disabled by the declaration by the puny individual of objection on the ground of conscience to any specific policy option adopted by his or her rulers. This freedom is inseparable from the idea of individualism. Neither is it inseparable from the idea of citizenship.

Does it mean that all or most who invoke conscientious objection are genuine or correct? By no means. But is the society better off allowing some charlatans to hide beneath this principle rather than wrongly coerce a single individual to go against her conscience? Obviously the answer is yes. This preference for the individual, the solicitousness on behalf of her well-being, is one aspect of individualism as a principle of social ordering that seems to upset Africans most. They can't understand why one individual's preference should trump those of the majority. As I indicated in the preceding discussion of communalism, the fact that many of my compatriots are not willing to entertain a debate about the merits of their preferred option is part of why I have gone out of my way to paint modernity in its most positive light.

A direct implication of the discussion so far is that we do not make rules or regulations that are designed to preempt action on the part of individuals; all that we are permitted is to make rules to take care of the contingency involved in their acting such that it injures another. It is why we do not impose punishment for thoughts: only the actions that are traceable to them warrant intervention. In the modern setting we not only require that the individual not be *prima facie* constrained in her acting; we disable other individuals, either in their individual capacity, or as groups both organised, e.g., the state, and unorganised from determining, without the individual's consent, how the individual should act or what she should do. In other words, we prohibit others, especially the state and government, from presuming to decide for the individual what course her life would take, what is the best life for her, and what is the most efficient route to its attainment.

When we say that the individual is sovereign, this is what we mean or should mean. She has an absolute freedom to form and seek to realise her own conception of the good life. We may be absolutely convinced that the individual is mistaken in the choices that she has made or that we can think of a better life for her than she has chosen. No matter, we are at liberty to counsel the individual on how she ought to go about leading her life; we are welcome to point out to her better ways of living; we may withdraw our friendship or association with her on account of the choices that she has made. But the fact that we are discomfited, disgusted, even horrified by her choices does not give us a warrant for interfering with her life or her plan for running it. Absent injury or the real threat of injury to another, not even the good of the individual permits us to thwart that individual's will once she has decided upon the course that her life will take.

This freedom to be whatever one chooses as long as one does not impair the ability of others with whom one shares a locale to do the same is the ultimate manifestation of the sovereignty of the individual that is a fundamental feature of the modern age. When we mouth all the platitudes regarding our respect for the individual, we are implicitly committed to guaranteeing this sovereignty and respecting it in all its ramifications. If there are some of these ramifications that we disagree with, we may not proceed—because we can—to outlaw them or make the transaction costs associated with their activation so expensive as to discourage the individual from embracing them. We must seek to persuade, possibly convince, but never coerce the individual to the superiority of our preferred ways. The less the activities concerned involve the welfare or interests of others, the less warranted is interference by others in an individual's life.

This sovereignty is best represented in the choices the individual makes in matters of adornment—hair, face, vestments, etc.—and how his or her personal space is arranged. When we make laws or enact regulations preempting how an individual should turn out in public or create an atmosphere in which it becomes acceptable to harass otherwise law-abiding individuals on account of what they are wearing, not only are we not respecting the individual concerned, we are in effect diminishing the individual's humanity on account of his or her nonconformity with our own standards of how one should look.

There is evidence that the humanity of our compatriots has been diminished in various countries across the African continent. There have been cases of women being assaulted in Kenya and Nigeria because they dared to wear trousers. One woman was jailed in Sudan for wearing trousers. A state governor in Nigeria ordered single women in his state to marry within a certain period or leave the boundaries of his state. The head of the Sharia police in Kano State, Nigeria once railed against a proposed march by divorced women in the state in support of their rights. His reason? It is "unIslamic" for divorced women to be heard and for women to march in public.

Yes, I know that opponents will argue that morality has to be protected and rules concerning indecency should be upheld. But, wait a minute. One of the other tenets of modernity that we alluded to above is a basic and deep-seated scepticism regarding morality and its injunctions. Precisely because of associated philosophical principles regarding the fallibility of our cognitive tools and the fact that reasonable people often disagree concerning the nature of and criteria for determining what is right and what is wrong, modern societies not only accommodate, they encourage heterogeneity where moral rules are concerned. It is why minimum moral rules are the vogue and much latitude is allowed for self-expression in private spaces and public spheres. It is why there are vigorous debates in them about indecency, pornography, and rape or other forms of unwarranted interference with or coercion of the will of another. When an actress is forced to flee and go into hiding for taking part in a sex scene in a video screened in Islam-dominated northern Nigeria or Christian zealots in southern Nigeria physically harass women for what the zealots consider unacceptable levels of exposure of female bodies, people like me must not only protest, we must pour scorn on such individuals' claims on behalf of individual dignity and respect for the person. Either they do not mean their professions or they do not have the slightest clue as to what such professions entail for their relations with their compatriots. When the Malian president was forced to backtrack on legislation requiring the equality of men and women in marriage, we have a clear case of not taking seriously our professed commitment to individual freedom. The vice chancellor of a state university in Nigeria declared in late 2010 that hugs, yes, hugs, between males and females are *haram,* that is, forbidden on his campus!

It gets worse. The apex of the education system—universities—that is supposed to chart the path to ever greater approximations to enlightened living in the modern age gets in the act of violating the individual in all the ways that we have mentioned and more. Dress codes are now in effect in most of the higher education institutions in Nigeria, a trend initiated by the parochial fundamentalist Christian universities that are proliferating in Nigeria. Some proprietors of some of the parochial and other private universities are convinced that they should become the moral police for their students up to and including, in the case of the newly-chartered Catholic university, having their students obtain exeats before they can venture out of the campus. The last time I remember anyone having to obtain permission to leave the school compound was when we were in boarding schools, primary and secondary. That secondary school students living away from home and away from the direct supervision of their parents might be compelled to operate within strict rules is quite consistent with the position that we have taken here. Few modern theorists aver that children fall under the category of individuals able to exercise rights and discharge the responsibilities attached to autonomous personhood. Given that we generally grant that the will in children is still in formation, we seek to direct young people along the path of what is considered upright in the society. What is more, the school assumes what is known as *in loco parentis* status relative to their wards and is answerable to the real parents for the safety and well-being of their children.

Universities are a different story. At least so I thought until the developments that I alluded to arose. They are supposed to be populated by adults who have minds of their own and can be counted upon to exercise their minds in ways that may be beneficial to all concerned, though that may not always be the case. And when the latter occurs, they are supposed to take responsibility for their actions or be held accountable for them. In seeking to curb the expression of their will or bend it to our own preferences, we are suggesting that university students' wills are as underdeveloped as those of high school students or that we do not have any regard for their autonomy and its associated privileges and forbearances. In short, we are abridging their individuality and not taking individualism seriously. Where do we stop?

Are we also going to tell university students who to vote for (they are old enough to vote) or to marry and when or if to have sex, how, and with whom?

Oftentimes, the import of what we have argued so far is lost on us as a people. Though our leaders struggled for independence, it is easy to forget the philosophical principles that informed their valiant efforts on behalf of freedom. They did not struggle just so that we today can have a flag of our own, a passport, and similar icons of our independence. Rather, the ultimate goal for which they and we strove was the right for us to be let alone, to determine the course of our collective lives, and to have, hold, and seek to attain our own conception of the good life. All we need do to realise the correctness of our affirmations is to remind ourselves that the fundamental hallmark of colonialism was the denial of the subjectivity of the colonised, the insistence of the coloniser on bending the will of the colonised to his purpose, and a stout refusal to countenance the possibility that the colonised may indeed prefer to live differently.

Those who fought and won the freedom struggle may not have realised the full import of the principles which guided their activities. They may have thought that all we wanted from the anti-colonial struggle was to be free to be Africans. But if what we have right now in the continent, some of which we have described in this work, is what it is to be Africans, please let me off this train! I insist that it is either the case that we have not fully apprehended or, if we have, embraced what the fuller implications of the underlying principles of our socio-political arrangements are. Our fighters all argued for self-determination. It seems that all and sundry understood self-determination only in the narrowest terms of the right of collectivities—ethnic groups, nations, etc. What is often forgotten or ignored is that self-determination is itself an extension to collectivities of the autonomy of individuals that we have been talking about. It is the individual's right writ large. It is their right within collectivities to be different: Heterodoxy rules!

I think the problem is that once independence was won, we thought that how we manage the individual-collective relationship within our independent societies no longer mattered or that, if it did, it might not be problematic. We proceeded to write laws, enact regulations, and generally create atmospheres in our communities in which the will of the individual amounts to little, if anything; in which we routinely subvert the autonomy of individuals; and in which we routinely discount the capacity of individuals to lead their lives as they see fit for what we erroneously think are more preferred gains for the collective well-being. When we are challenged we are quick to point out that Africans are, by nature, communalistic; that the group is everything and that however much we value the individual, we cannot allow the wish, interest, or welfare of the individual to trump those of the community.

No thanks to our unthinking preference for communalism, we do not organise our societies to take full advantage of the modern idea of individualism. It is no surprise that most African states have no decent systems for levying and collecting taxes. The truth of the matter is: "communities pay tributes; individuals pay taxes." If you cannot reach individuals, your tax system in the modern age is likely to be inefficient and incapable of reaching most of your citizenry. No thanks to our morbid fascination with a quaint but dated communalism, we inhabit cities with no character. Few are our cities with identities; it is rare to find art dedicated to celebrating the individual character of our cities. Because there is no competition amongst them, there is rarely to be found the kinds of "self-love" that characterise the great cities of the world and their peculiar ways, music, art, food, neighbourhoods or sights. Other cities, even poor ones, build monuments to awe their competition and enhance their standing in the world, perhaps in history; we build slums and nondescript structures. How often have African cities held global competitions to get the best human minds to help design our spaces and build feasts of beauty for our local eyes and those of outsiders?

It is why we do not hold as a goal individual ownership of dwellings on a mass scale complete with individualised essential services. It is why local governments are forever wasting time on so-called communal projects like "wells and public water taps." Notice the wide availability of individually owned homes with modern conveniences does not stop individualist societies from providing public versions of same without proclaiming their "communal" character. This may also explain why, in part, we do not think of the convenience of individuals when we design and operate our public facilities, especially toilets and similar facilities. We often don't provide them. Might it be because we think no one would refuse another the use of facilities in their home or business? And when we do, we do not do so with a view to ensuring comparative comfort for individuals. Again, however much we are invested in community it is as lone individuals that we experience, for good and ill, the provision of these facilities.

Our attachment to *faux* communalism does not mean, as I pointed out, that we do not copy from individualist societies. We do. The problem is that we are quite selective in our choice of what to copy from those societies from which the preponderant percentage of our current institutions, processes and practices are drawn. I do not begrudge us the right to be so selective. In fact, the guarantee of this right to be different is singularly characteristic of the modern age. The difficulty is that, to be consistent, we must recognise the extendability of this right to all areas and levels of life. Its true import lies in the recognition of the right of husbands to differ with and from their wives; the same for parents and their children; bosses and their subordinates; among co-workers, siblings, friends, and so on. Instead, we insist that we do not need to go the whole hog because we are different.

Our scholars are ever ready to trot out innumerable specious justifications for why Africa is so different from the land, temperament, and peoples from whom we drew our original inspiration towards modernity, that we must always find a way to elude what we consider the worst excesses of those societies. Africans love to be different. Let me rephrase that. African intellectuals, in or out of leadership positions, in all spheres of human endeavour, love to be different. They revel in it; they wallow in it. They kill for it; they die for it. Nothing makes them happier than when others, especially peoples of Caucasian extraction, mark, set apart, and work within the parameters set by this radical difference of Africans from other human beings. And any attempt, like the present one, to dismiss difference or diminish its significance as a marker of African identity is often apprehended by African intellectuals as a declaration of hostilities, an acknowledgment on the part of the one who advances it that he is a victim of colonial mentality or, worse, a self-hater who has lost or is uncomfortable with who he is and is trying to pass as someone else.

The tragedy is that these rather boisterous proclaimers of African difference are completely unaware of the ironies that abound in their existential situation. In the first place, they are more likely than not proclaiming their difference in non-native languages of European provenance. So much for difference. Secondly, the difference template that they so eagerly use to configure their identity did not have its origins in Africa or in African minds. It was racist Europeans who wished to find a justification for denying the common humanity of Africans who authored the original thesis of the radical difference of the African. The irony is deeper still when one explores the manner in which ordinary Africans, especially our forebears, accounted for Europeans at the earliest time of contact. I think that it is fair to suggest that Africans did not and could not have originally related to their European visitors in terms of difference. Had they done so, they probably would not have welcomed them into their midst. I am suggesting that if they did, it could not have been on the basis of a radical idea of difference.

Much of the metaphysics that one finds in many African philosophical systems is committed to the basic unity of humankind. Europeans were different humans, but humans nonetheless. Europeans were welcomed by Africans more in terms of their common humanity, and the boundaries of much of the idea of human nature in Africa were structured to account for this fact. That Africans later found out that they were mistaken in their estimation of their guests had less to do with the humanity of their guests but with the latter's cultural preferences, especially their ethics. It was as a part of the guests' ethics that they denied the common humanity they shared with their African hosts, whom they would later turn into their slaves and, subsequently, under colonialism, their wards. The absolute difference of the African was forged from this racist template. It is instructive that the first Africans who were present at the inauguration of this pernicious discourse vigorously disputed and combated it. They used their indigenous knowledge they garnered from Euro-American educational institutions and their participation in the intellectual culture fostered by modernity to refute all characterisations of the African as somewhat less than human.

Unfortunately, since the colonial era, so steeped in colonialist assumptions and so indolent have African intellectuals become that we have embraced "difference" as our way of being in the human community. Our identity is not defined by what we are but by what we are not. By focusing too much on what makes us different, we have neglected to take hold of solutions that have worked for other humans and apply them to problems that plague us, too. By contrast, Indian intellectuals made modernity their own so much they reinvented it for the world, including the Euro-American world in the last third of the twentieth century and have used its economic component—capitalism—to catapult India into a global powerhouse. The Chinese decided in 1976 that their people are no different from the rest of humanity and can use better paying jobs, more creature comforts, and overall just a higher standard of living and proceeded to free up the energies and imagination of their teeming population to accelerate their movement towards modernity. South Korea, at its founding, decided that modernity offered its population a one-way ticket out of the well in which, as Koreans used to describe themselves, they were all crabs pulling one another down. Singapore, Malaysia, Brazil, Spain, Hungary, countries big and small, multiculturally diverse with histories right across the spectrum from monarchy to totalitarianism, have all made similar choices.

Where is Africa in all this? NOWHERE! Given our difference, we feel no shame that we have pretty much become the only beggar continent left in the world. Our mendicant rulers and their intellectual enablers have no difficulty accepting alms from countries that, not too long ago, were with us holding out their alms bowls with outstretched hands. Witness India now becoming a foreign aid donor to Africa; the same with Ireland and South Korea. Needless to say, we don't feel any shame because we don't see anything wrong with our situation. Given that we are radically different, it is our lot to be poor, underfed, unhealthy, and just generally backward. It is our portion to be helped and sustained by the generosity of others.

The mantra of difference obscures the uncomfortable facts yielded by focusing on our shared humanity. Think of it: if we dared to compare ourselves with common humanity, not embrace shibboleths offered by cheap anti-westernism, we would quickly discover how low we have sunk on all scales of human living standards. What if, instead of accepting that Liberia deserves to be inferior to the United States, we compare Liberia and Costa Rica? If the BBC's country profiles can be believed, Liberia and Costa Rica should not be too far apart in the fortunes of their respective peoples. Yet, they are so far apart one might be spooked into thinking that they must be radically different from each other. For one thing, they are both rain forest countries. Costa Rica preserves its forest and earns substantial revenues from ecotourism; Liberia risks losing its forest to loggers in the nearest future. Costa Rica's population is 4.5 million; Liberia's is 3.9 million. Life expectancy for men in Costa Rica is 76 years and for women, 81 years. What are the equivalents for Liberia? 57 years for men; 59 years for women. The gross national income per capita for Costa Rica is $6,060 in 2008 figures, that of Liberia is $170. It is even more intriguing when one looks at the main exports of both countries. For Costa Rica, they are coffee, bananas, sugar, textiles, electronic components, and electricity; for Liberia, diamonds, iron ore, rubber, timber, coffee, and cocoa. Why are the fortunes of the two countries so divergent given their similarities? And they are both ex-colonies, to boot! Why did Liberian intellectuals collaborate with Master Sergeant Samuel Doe and later did business with the thug, Charles Taylor, and Costa Ricans, on the contrary, used the occasion of a coup d'état to abolish the army entirely? Why do African intellectuals find it easy to sing the praises of nincompoops who dominate our public life when they should have given fight or refrain from cooperating? Similar comparisons can be made of, say, Chile and Zambia; Ethiopia and Philippines; Brazil and Nigeria; and so on. If we would compare ourselves with others, rather than differentiate ourselves from them, we might be shamed into action that will move us forward with the rest of humanity.

Were we no different from the rest of common humanity, we would be more inclined, maybe even compelled, to embrace the same solutions that have worked for our fellow members of the human family across variegated historical, social, cultural, and political boundaries. We would feel outrage at our continuing prostrate position while the rest of the world has moved on and left us behind. We would react negatively to leaders and intellectuals who wish to preserve the continent as a museum and our peoples and cultures as artefacts of what the racists always have insisted is "the infancy of the human race." We would strive to break the shackles that our leaders and intellectuals put us in, all the better for them to enjoy the fleshpots of modernity in their repeated forays into modern lands, even as they do their utmost best to frighten us from embracing modern values, institutions, and processes and becoming positively contaminated in so doing.

My problem, though, is that in our selective choosing of what to emulate at the present time from the western world, from which originate our core institutions, we are not choosing those ideas and practices that help those societies become the cynosure of all eyes around the world and the object of attraction for African immigrants who are willing to risk life and limb to live in them. It would not be an appropriate response to say that African immigrants only want the material prosperity that the Euro-American world promises. Far from it, the reason that both Nobel laureates and drug smugglers alike seek to lead their lives in those shores is the promise of control over their individual lives that living there promises.

I once had a conversation with a Nigerian friend whom I was trying to convince of the persuasiveness of the case that I am making in this book. I had asked him whether he or I or quite a number of us who now make our homes in Euro-America went to those countries because we were lured by the promise of regular power, water, and food supplies and stayed because of the bright lights and other material comforts that our countries of sojourn offer. He answered, no. The reason for this is not far to seek. Indeed if what we desired were merely material comforts, many of us now in Euro-America would probably be in a position to procure those things at the individual level in Africa, as do most of our compatriots who stay home, even when the state remains remiss in discharging those functions. A good part of the reason that we immigrated to Euro-America, I suggested and my friend agreed, relates to the opportunity that their countries offer for self-realisation and, more importantly, more control over the course of our lives and those of our offspring, especially in areas of choosing our rulers, deciding how we lead our lives "from the inside," and having our personal spaces respected, if not treated with utter sanctity. I suspect that many of those who may offer the objections that I have been considering fall within the same demographic group as my friend and me. They are the ones who do not miss any opportunity to come to Euro-America to, as one of them said to us several years ago, "get some fresh air." Here is my challenge: why is it okay for members of our upper and middle classes, such as they are, to help themselves to the intangible but more significant rewards of modernity while they object to making the same available to the lowliest of their compatriots in African countries?

THREE

The Knowledge Society and Its Rewards

What does it mean to free the mind and cultivate it? In liberal education, the recipients are put through their paces by being exposed to the best and finest that the human mind has produced through the history of human civilisation.

I WOULD like to begin with three anecdotes that, I hope, would set the context for the discussion to follow in this chapter. Several years ago, I was lecturing a class at Ifẹ̀, and I was trying to impress on my students the importance of pursuing knowledge for its own sake. I used for my illustration a scientist studying fish psychology. Of course, my students did not think much of my example. Why, they wondered, would anyone be interested in that? What purpose would it serve? Certainly, they were in no doubt that such an engagement would be a waste of the scientist's time and talent as well as of the resources that the society concerned has invested in both the university where he or she works and the training of the scientist.

For literally all the years that we spent together in graduate school my very good friend, a political scientist, used to remind me, jocoseriously, that I was involved with a useless discipline, philosophy, which, according to him, "does not grow food." Finally, not too long ago, I was at a philosophy conference where one of the presenters read a paper lamenting the fate of philosophy in an African country in which, according to the speaker, philosophy has rendered itself irrelevant because its practitioners treat issues that do not speak to the quotidian concerns of the populace. The panacea for the situation, the speaker concluded, is for philosophy to get out in the world, treat practical concerns, and offer solutions to real problems.

What comes across clearly from the three situations just described is that any intellectual pursuit that does not promise results, immediate, or remote, that impact the daily experience of ordinary people, or that represent solutions to real problems in the real world is not worthy of our energies or, at a minimum, should not dominate our energies as scholars. The mindset that is reflected in this insistence on results is widely distributed in the continent and, I would argue, is the best indication that we in Africa lack one of the essential attributes of the modern age: modern society is a "society of knowledge," as one of its foremost philosophers once put it. It is one in which knowledge is pursued, supported, funded, and embraced for its own sake. That is, it is the type of society in which just knowing is what is valued and putting what one knows to some use is often incidental or obliquely realised. Yes, modern society does make use of its knowledge to make things, grow food, and generally mass produce the creature comforts and gadgets that Africans, including intellectuals, are all too content to rack up debts and sometimes trade off their self-respect to acquire. But the primary motivation for pursuing knowledge is simply to push back knowledge's frontiers. This is related to the modern tenet respecting the centrality of Reason and its deployment in the conquest of Nature, of both the world around us and the one inside us.

Let us examine the above anecdotes a little more closely. The person who wishes to study fish behaviour may be motivated by nothing more than sheer curiosity and a burning desire to add to our knowledge of fish and their characteristics. We can imagine the scholar putting together her application for funding from appropriate agencies. We shall be making a lot more of this requirement of sponsorship for scholarship anon. If she were to follow the requirement of showing what practical problems would be solved by her investigation, it is highly unlikely that her idea would ever take off. After all, she did not get the idea from seeing fish die off in the large numbers that might provoke a need to explain why such an event was occurring. In societies where "I would like to expand the frontiers of our knowledge of fish" is a legitimate and often sufficient reason for attracting fund-ing, as long as the design of her project is vetted and approved by her peers, and is held to meet the standards that are considered requisite for making her proposed re-search viable, she would most likely be funded.

Now there is no reason to believe that the con-ditions in such a society would be much different from those in ours—scarcity of resources, competing demands for them, social problems that require solutions, etc. So, the society concerned is not paying the scientist to have the time and leisure that are requisite for her work be-cause it is so well off that it can afford to fund its scholars' whimsies. It is that such a society has decided that the expansion of knowledge is a good that it desires to have and, hence, sponsor.

Meanwhile, there are no guarantees that what would come of the research will solve any practical prob-lems. Indeed, it may be the case that the scientist would find out that "fish don't behave at all." Yet, even such a finding will become a part of the repertoire of knowledge of that society and instruct future investigators to look in other directions. Nevertheless, one cannot discount the possibility of a more usable outcome. It may turn out that the sexual behaviour of fish is affected by some chemical imbalance in their brains, in the water they live in, or by changes in the temperature of the water. One can easily see how such a finding about fish that never make it to our dinner tables might tell us something about the re-productive patterns of those that do. Right there, we have a solution to a problem that was not even a part of the original reason for conducting the research.

A society that insists that its scholars, to merit sponsorship, career advancement, and/or recognition only or mainly do research that relates one way or another to practical problems is a society that is not likely to be in the ranks of those who expand the frontiers of knowledge. They may do so but only in an indirect way. Requiring that its scholars be firmly tethered to problem solving, given that not even the most advanced societies are without problems screaming for solutions, such a society's thinkers are unlikely to display the rich, fecund imagination that reaches out to ideas, issues, and problems that have not even been apprehended. The cramping of the scholarly imagination, the limitation placed on the freedom to think about anything and everything, and the refusal to underwrite the leisure that is a prerequisite for sustained intellectual work can only result in the kinds of universities that now dominate the African landscape, many of which are, to put it mildly, glorified diploma mills. I shall explain later why this must necessarily be the case.

To my friend who insisted that the study of philosophy is useless because "it does not grow food," I have since definitively rejoined that neither does political science nor any of the disciplines that make up both the liberal arts and the pure sciences. To limit myself to philosophy, I pointed out to him that growing food may be the easier question to answer: after all, food grows in the wild without anyone tending it. Of greater significance may be—and in the contemporary world, it increasingly is—the question of whether or not we should grow food, what food we should grow and in what quantities, how and where food should be grown, and who should have what quantity of what is grown and with what frequency. The latter set of questions cannot be answered by agricultural science; but how they are answered may impact the lives and fortunes of many and the fate of our planet. These are preeminently philosophical questions whose answers require that we delve into what to many are the murky waters of metaphysics, epistemology and axiology. Yet these are not disciplines that are tied to specific "practical problems" or, at least, they are not so tied immediately.

It is time to draw out the larger implications of the analysis of our anecdotes. Recall what was said above about how a speaker felt that in order for philosophy to make itself relevant, it should engage problems of practical concern to a country whose peoples are interested in development and nation-building. But, and this is the line that I wish to pursue in the rest of this discussion, to insist on the speaker's point is to misconstrue what philosophy and the other disciplines in the liberal arts and sciences are meant to be and do. I limit myself to the fortunes of philosophy. Having grown tired of the snide responses of questioners to my announcement since graduate school that I study philosophy, I now introduce myself to all and sundry, especially the students that I have been privileged to teach in various countries, as a "peddler of useless knowledge." By putting this forward before they challenge me to persuade them that I am not just an unredeemed and unrecoverable expense on the society's coffers, I preempt their response. The payoff is that over the years, I have had the occasional chance to have useful conversations with those who are intrigued by my description and have gone away less befuddled by the peculiar character of the pure arts, the bedrock of a liberal education.

What I say of philosophy is true of all the other disciplines in the university except those in the professional schools. As I always love to tease my students who claim they are not philosophy majors because they cannot think of what to do with it post graduation, and then declare for sociology, political science, or psychology instead, not a single one of those alternatives escapes the fate of philosophy: they are one and all embodiments of useless knowledge if usefulness is to be measured by whether or not being schooled in them will equip their graduates to make things. A degree in sociology does not make its recipient a sociologist; the same is true of a degree in physics and a physicist or in mathematics and a mathematician.

When properly understood and correctly executed, a liberal education—both arts and sciences—is not an education in making things; or, at least, not directly. An education in making things is the proper province of vocational and technical schools dedicated to the inculcation of the skills requisite for the industrial and mechanical arts. By saying this, I do not mean to suggest that one type of education is superior to the other. I am merely registering the key differentia in a pure arts-driven liberal education and a vocational one. The primary purpose of a liberal education is to free the mind or intellect and, having freed it, cultivate it. Certainly, there is no suggestion here that this only takes place in the university. The truth of our claim can be found in the fact that many who do not have the benefit of a university education and others who start out in vocational fields but end up as great intellectuals, hardly fail to point out that their successes are often built on a deep passion for and disinterested pursuit of knowledge that, at the time of their pursuit, could not be said to have held any promise of producing results beyond that of expanding their minds.

What does it mean to free the mind and cultivate it? In liberal education, the recipients are put through their paces by being exposed to the best and finest that the human mind has produced through the history of human civilisation. That is why they are schooled in the classics of various human civilisations, the most abstruse accretions of mathematics, physics, and chemistry, not to talk of the most recondite of human achievements in music and other art forms. Whether in philosophy or in art, in sociology or in political science, the aim is not to impart techniques of how to fabricate things. Rather the effort is always geared to enabling its recipients to come to understand the principle of things, the laws of their operation: how they work and why they work the way they do, what they are, and so on.

The reader can now see why the wider the scope covered—one meaning of the word liberal—the better the education promises to be. We do not make the recipients denizens of these exciting mindscapes without simultaneously asking, or minimally encouraging, them to explore the boundary with unrestrained enthusiasm and unfettered imagination. We encourage them to mix and match, combine uncombinables, seek to unite conflicting perspectives, all with the aim of learning even from those syntheses that do not work, why they don't and those that do, why they do. Hence, the repeated practice of the mind seeking to push back the frontiers of knowledge is what the cultivation of the intellect entails.

When we demand of our scholars that they only engage in research motivated primarily by the need to solve practical problems, we put curbs on their imagination. The free spirit that a liberal education is meant to foster becomes caged or its wings are clipped. Yes, it is okay to solve problems that we have identified. But there are problems that lurk and have yet to come to the surface. What problem would we immediately be solving by spending money to find out what enables migratory birds to make the extremely long journeys required to enable them to move from one end of the globe to another? Or the mating patterns of particular birds, say, penguins? There are dimensions of extant problems that are not immediately palpable. There may be ways to conceptualise existing problems which are unearthed by linking them to themes and concerns that are not immediately related to them. The possibilities just sketched are what make a liberal education and the pursuit of useless knowledge, with the freedom to roam that comes with it, such a bedrock of discoveries in the arts and the sciences that shape our lives and make them and our world infinitely more livable.

Had there not been this commitment to the cultivation of a free spirit of inquiry, science would have been impossible and great achievements in the humanities would not have become such standard fare in human civilisations. I am arguing that at the base of that development in the so-called advanced countries after which African countries hanker and which they are desirous of replicating was the knowledge society that modernity inaugurated and which led to the scientific revolution and, later, the industrial revolution. I know I would be reminded of the role played by the Trans-Atlantic Slave Trade, Colonialism and Neocolonialism in the emergence and sustenance of Euro-American wealth. I am not denying this nor does my thesis require that I deny it. I am less concerned with how the wealth came about than I am with what use the wealth was put to. It was not all the countries that profited from the above phenomena that went on to become significant players in the two revolutions at issue here. Think Spain; think Portugal. The template was marked by that modern tenet regarding the centrality of Reason, the overthrow of faith, authority and tradition as sources and validations of knowledge claims. The freeing of the intellect which made Albert Einstein eventually dare to proclaim that the ultimate goal of his research is to "know the mind of God" made the pursuit of knowledge an end in itself and what use it could serve of only secondary importance.

That maniacal pursuit of knowledge is what informs the foundation, structure, and operation of the modern university. Universities are defined by their being universes of knowledge where the pursuit of knowledge in its multiversity is their fundamental reason for being. This is the principal reason that the world's most reputable universities, even those set up as institutes of technology, are founded on the solid pylons of core colleges of liberal arts and sciences. Examples include the Massachusetts Institute of Technology, California Institute of Technology, University of California-Berkeley, and Harvard University, all in the United States. It is not unusual to find in them students who combine studies in religion with those in physics, biology majors who are minoring in music, mathematics graduates who are headed for law school, and philosophy majors who are headed for medical school after graduation. They are home to the kind of an informal group of physicists at the University of Chicago who get together during their lunch breaks to talk and theorise about the physics of liquid coffee spills on table-tops and other surfaces. Just as in the case of the earlier illustration of the fish behaviour research, should the physicists here end up with some significant finding respecting the trajectory of spills, one can see how that might have some spinoff in the areas of fabric design and dry cleaning or even in forensics.

A close look at the interests of the Nobel Prize winners of 2008 and at what led them to their path-breaking researches confirms what we claim here. The chemistry prize winner, for example, was attracted by glowing fish and wanted to figure out what is responsible for their phosphorescence. What they all shared in common, including the literature prize winner, was investigating what interested them the most; it was not the usability of the results that motivated them. For example, the discovery that eventually led to the development of Viagra had absolutely nothing to do with the male anatomy at its inception; it was a product of serendipity and only later did its possible application to erectile dysfunction become apparent. Nor did those who worked on the sensors that are now powering garage doors think that automatically-operated door openers were a priority when they were doing their work. There is no need to multiply examples.

Do our countries aspire to knowledge society status? Sadly, this question can only be answered in the negative. I cannot talk about the genealogy of universities in the non-anglophone African countries. But it is fair to say that in the anglophone countries, their universities did not emerge as organic growths from a social formation suffused with the tenets of modernity, the most relevant of which to our discussion we already mentioned above: the centrality of Reason. Our universities are not set up with the primary purpose of pushing back the frontiers of knowledge. They were instead set up as manufactories for manpower development, initially in the service of the colonial economy and, later, for the project of nation-building and rapid economic development. In other words, they were not set up, chartered, as the apex institutions of a mode of knowledge production where the production, distribution, and consumption of knowledge are the prime reason for being.

This may explain why African universities hardly ever feature in all the lists of reputable and top institutions. This point bears repeating for, in recent years, to take just one example, there has been a lot of hyperventilating about the absence of Nigerian universities from the list of the top 500 universities in the world. One professor said that the reason that no Nigerian institution made the list was that Nigerian schools are not present enough on the Internet and many of them do not have websites that report the accomplishments of their faculty. This, by itself, is an indictment of our institutions supposedly operating in the modern age. The lack of commitment to knowledge leads them to a failure on their part to produce and disseminate knowledge about what they do to the outside world. Incidentally, the same flaw afflicts even our governments all across the continent. Another offered in a public lecture that the country's universities will need about ₦125bn or some such humongous amount to attain world class status.

It is amusing how often African intellectuals love to lament the lack of resources and blame it for their failures to discharge their roles in society. What they often miss or choose to ignore is that many African universities have not always suffered from the lack of resources affliction. Time was when they were few and their countries' resources were not as badly stretched as they are nowadays. The question is: did African universities back then make the grade? Did they feature in the world's top lists even then? Most important of all, why didn't African scholars create a university system built to withstand the buffetings of the inclement political and economic weather that has since become a dominant feature of African life? The explanation may be found, in part, in the structural defects at their inception.

I believe that once we move away from the grandstanding and grandiose claims that African scholars love to make—at par with the elaborate academic vestments we love to wear, none of which is traceable to any of our indigenous heritages, to hide the sheer emptiness of our intellectual and ideational treasuries—the reality of the situation is much uglier. For us to begin the gigantic task of reconstruction that our situation calls for, it is vital that we first acknowledge that ours has never been a knowledge society of the type under discussion here. The point needs to be made. Nothing that I say here is meant to suggest that African societies do not produce knowledge or that we only obtained or created knowledge after the alien historical movements had irrupted into our lives.

In not being a knowledge society, we are like the rest of humanity, including European humanity, before the arrival of the modern age. In order for us to become one we must commit to fostering the deployment of Reason, which we have in abundance as a banal part of our sheer humanity, in all that we do. "In all that we do" is the key phrase. Rather than moving forward, in the last two decades or so, our societies have traded in even that semblance of a commitment to the centrality of reason for a fervid embrace of the most retrograde, reason-averse versions of Christianity and Islam.

Again, our universities and their products have been in the forefront of this slide into irrationality. It was bad enough in the past that we were not a knowledge society; it is now much worse that we are fast turning into an actively, virulently anti-knowledge society. At the present time, from our political leaders to our professors, our sportswomen and men to our artists, no one achieves success any more by dint of hard work, but everything now is owed to God's glory! By the same token, most of life's processes, including the causes of events, especially disasters—natural and contrived—are assigned to God's inscrutable will. It should by now be clear why, in the current era that has witnessed an explosion in the sheer numbers of universities and other tertiary institutions as well as of graduates in all spheres of African life, the continent continues to sink deeper and deeper into the morass of superstition and supernaturalism.

While we are busy digging our way back furiously to the Dark Ages, other societies that used to be like us are busy distancing themselves as they accelerate towards becoming knowledge societies. A few years ago, Malaysia allocated $571 million to seed a nascent biogenetic sector to enable the country to become a participant in the burgeoning field of genetic science. The scandal over the Korean scientist who overreached himself in stem cell research has not cooled the ardour of Korea for moving along nicely on the path to scientific supremacy. Any one who has been following the vagaries of stem cell research knows that there are no guarantees that any or most of the research would yield any usable results. But that has not stopped societies that take the pursuit of knowledge seriously from ploughing huge amounts of funds into work in the area.

Korea now leads the world in research and development of flat screen display technology. We are happy enough to deplete our foreign exchange reserves buying the monitors they are installed in. Singapore is busy challenging Switzerland in the area of banking; Dubai and Qatar are investing for the day when oil dries up and they are opening their societies up to knowledge. South Korea is now a full member of the Organisation for Economic Cooperation and Development. They did not all come by their current status by building artisanal workshops in lieu of universities. Unfortunately, our countries, after killing our universities, are now busy sending our graduate students to Korea for training as part of Korean foreign aid to countries like Uganda and Kenya.

I would not like to be misunderstood. I am not suggesting that only scientific knowledge counts. Quite the contrary, knowledge societies seek to acquire knowledge of everything, and they do not believe that any area is disqualified from being a candidate for rational investigation. Hence they encourage their scholars, students, intellectuals, and sundry other investigators—amateurs, experts, dabblers, professionals—to seek, record, store, disseminate, process, and retrieve knowledge, not because there are practical problems to be solved but simply because it is good to know! At the top of this intellectual food chain are the universities. You have in their ranks those who study big things; others who study small things. You have those who do multi-year, multi-segment, multi-volume research, and you have those who study one thing for a very long time and become, as the saying goes, "the world's foremost authority" on the subject-matter of their exertions. We used to have knowledge producers like that. Many of them have become exiles (about which, see below); others have surrendered to "Jesus" or "Mohammed PBOH." Thanks to the profusion of knowledge producers in knowledge societies there is no area of life in these societies that lacks its complement of knowledge seekers; no topic is too light, no theme too simple for knowledge of it to be sought, harvested, stored, and disseminated.

This is not the case with African universities. Given what we said above regarding their origins, it is not surprising that they are barely above the level of vocational training schools where the overarching concern is to train manpower for economic development and nation-building. Certainly, there are experts in numerous areas. But it will be a stretch to say that African scholars form a continuum with an intelligentsia that includes amateur historians, sociologists, musicologists, herbologists, and so on. Hence, it is unlikely that we'll find resident in our universities experts on the micro details of city politics in any of our major metropolises. There is a disconnection between our universities and their locations. No one thinks of tapping expertise from them for local problems. They themselves are too busy talking beyond their borders while neglecting their local hosts. We explain why this is so momentarily.

Take a city like Ibadan, for instance. It is a storied city which has been the setting for some of the most significant events that have shaped the history of contemporary Nigeria in many areas. In the area of politics, it is widely acknowledged that the immediate trigger of the chain of events that culminated in Nigeria's first military coup d'état took place in the city. The event that some have erroneously claimed flagged off the injection of tribalism into Nigerian politics took place in the city. Ibadan was the location for the abductions and assassinations that were pivotal to the second military coup in July 1966. One would think that given the examples just iterated, the University of Ibadan and others in what we may call Ibadan's catchment area—Ago Iwoye, Abeokuta, Ile-Ife, Iwo, Oyo—would have in their ranks scholars who make it their lives' work studying in their extreme microscopic details these elements of Ibadan politics and history. I dare anyone to point to such a faculty member at any of those institutions.

There is more. Ibadan was home to the Mbari Club. It was where Wole Soyinka and Ulli Beier called home for a long time. It was where Chinua Achebe, Christopher Okigbo, Demas Nwoko, J.P. Clark, Mabel Segun, Duro Ladipo, Kola Ogunmola, and a host of lesser known but no less distinguished contributors to the development of arts and letters in Africa resided and worked. Again, do we have historians, sociologists, philosophers, and other scholars who make this aspect of Ibadan history the object of their intellectual strivings? Ibadan, as far as I know, does not even have a historical society; has no bodies for historical preservation; and hosts no archivists of its intellectual and material artefacts: in short, no intellectual considers it worth their professional lives to make the microscopic study of life in a modern historic megalopolis the object of their scholarly engagement.

Were Nigeria a knowledge society, things would be different. In the first place, Ibadan would have a community of intellectuals who are seized of the city's importance in history, fascinated by life as it is led by various groups within it, desirous of recording for posterity the goings on in it, committed to tracking and elucidating changing trends in it from food to fashion, architecture to commerce, language to music, and numerous other themes. There will be ongoing controversies and debates about land use and changes in the landscape: for example, whether or not old Dùgbẹ̀ Market should be preserved or dismantled; the many changes around the old "red light districts" of Èkótẹ̀dó Ìyá Ọlọ́bẹ̀ and Ògùnpa Èkó; the history of floods [*omíyalé*] in the city, not to mention the changing character of its numerous neighbourhoods in the course of time. In short, Ibadan should sustain an incredibly large knowledge industry complete with newspapers, books, journals, media establishments, and a whole coterie of commentators, critics, artists, performers, and so on.

If what I have just said of Ibadan is accepted, can you imagine what it would be like in a Nigeria—or Ghana, Kenya, Senegal, or Angola—in which the above scenario (where the cities become the foci of intellectual engagement of the sort just described) is replicated for all of Nigeria's biggest centres of population? Remember that our interest is in the production, distribution and consumption of knowledge across a broad spectrum. Yet there is no doubting that such a proliferation promises salubrious consequences for other areas of life, especially that of the economy. What is more, we would have available and on call a battery of experts who can shed light on events as they occur and free us from that racist script in which African suffering is always explained by the ubiquitous lone wolf white expert who has adopted for his or her life's work the study of whichever benighted African people is the flavour of the moment in the foreign media. I don't think that I need to spell out what it would be like to replicate the model across the continent.

The losses that accrue from our not being a knowledge society are gargantuan, yet hardly visible, much less acknowledged. As a primary school pupil growing up in Ibadan, I watched as a younger cousin of mine failed to walk at an appropriate age. His mother, my father's niece, did the rounds of indigenous healers, Christian prophets, Muslim seers, and sundry other help to diagnose what was wrong with the child. She eventually ended up at the University College Hospital, Ibadan, (another storied institution that deserves scholarly attention), where the poor child was diagnosed with polio. I was too young to have weighed in. But the episode did not escape my apprehension.

Fast forward to several years later by which time I was studying for my Higher School Certificate and my aunt's daughter, too, was not walking when she was supposed to have learnt to. My aunt, too, was doing the usual round of seeking the malevolent dark forces who were sitting on her daughter's limbs and would not allow her to rise up and walk. Her situation was more delicate because she was married then to a self-proclaimed Senior Apostle of the Cherubim and Seraphim Church. Her daughter's condition was not improving. Then, one day, I went to visit her at her shop, adjacent to her sister's, my mother, during a vacation from boarding school. I had lived with my aunt for sometime when I was still a toddler, so there had always been a special relationship between us. She was also like a mother to me. That day, something snapped inside me. My mind went back to the earlier case of my other cousin who had been afflicted with polio as an infant and how delay in seeking a correct diagnosis and appropriate treatment meant that he walks with a pronounced limp even now. By then, too, thanks to my education, I knew what polio was and guessed that my cousin's affliction might be another case. I went to my aunt and literally ordered her, on pain of a permanent rupture in our relations should she refuse, no later than the following morning to the same hospital that had treated the earlier case to have their doctors check out her daughter, my cousin. Unsurprisingly, the diagnosis was polio. Because her limb had not degenerated as badly as in the earlier case, her limp is not as pronounced or noticeable. Who knows what remedial measures might have been available had she been taken to the hospital sooner.

I have told the above story to indicate the power of knowledge even from a lowly 17-year-old who knew and continues to embrace the maxim: knowledge is power. I am sure many readers will find equivalent stories in their own lives. In our various countries at the present time, fewer and fewer among us academics seem to care for this maxim. We are living in changed and changing times. These changes affect all areas of our lives. Our work habits have changed. What we eat has changed radically. The arrangement of our physical space has altered beyond belief. Our architecture, even in the remotest of hamlets, no longer bears any semblance to forms indigenous to us through our history. How we govern ourselves has also altered beyond recognition. Meanwhile our scholars lament every day the awful fate awaiting our original cultures, especially our native languages. The ways in which we used to conceptualise illness and good health have been drastically altered and our dominant orientation these days is a mish-mash of indigenous influences and alien traditions.

We have indigenised Islam, Christianity and embraced motley other religious and spiritual traditions. Our indigenous religious traditions in many parts of the continent have not for that reason gone away. Although African philosophy has earned its place as a sub-discipline of philosophy, slim indeed are the pickings where substantive philosophical works are concerned which are rooted in the cultural idioms domiciled across the continent. The flora and fauna of the continent are studied more by outsiders than by Africans themselves. There are more non-Africans taking scholarly interests in African art forms—visual, performing, and plastic—than Africans. And the more obscure the art form or the more closely tied to its indigenous roots, the greater the likelihood that it will not be studied much by scholars whose form it is.

In a knowledge society, its intellectuals would be seized of the tremendous opportunities for knowledge production, distribution, consumption, processing, retrieval, and dissemination presented by the widespread changes just described. We would have books, monographs, journals, workshops, conferences, colloquia, seminars, etc., looking at all aspects of life through the many changes at different historical periods, tracking them in the minutest details. I can imagine exciting debates drawing in old academics and young ones, freshly-minted Ph.D.s and bright graduate students, journalists who would be contributing from their vantage point in the media even as they are reporting on the latest discoveries and controversies among researchers. Undergraduate students will have the privilege of sharing, through participation, in the excitement of knowledge production. High and primary school pupils won't be left out because the culture of inquiry will, with time, percolate to those levels, too, and we shall have young people aspiring to careers as researchers from a very young age. We may even look forward to magazines that seek to present scientific findings to an audience of discerning general readers who are curious and are capable of being so informed.

Notice that all we have said has been described without any concern whatsoever for so-called practical problems or manpower development or nation-building. What commends them to us is the fact that they are all activities designed to enhance our knowledge of ourselves, our environment, both physical and social, the nature of things, and so on. Will there be a pay off for "practical problems," "manpower development," and "nation-building"? There is absolutely no doubt. For one thing, many of our best and brightest who now have to take their gifts in biology, chemistry, or mathematics to banking, law, accounting, and allied fields, will have reason to stay closer to their natural endowments and by so doing enhance the possibility of doing top-flight scientific work right there in Africa. The need for support staff—technical and administrative—and for ancillary professionals—editors, printers, graphic artists—not to talk of firms making and supplying chemical reagents, laboratory equipment, and expertise as well as the manufacture and supply of stationery and office furniture and machines are bound to create more jobs than current practices can ever do.

I am suggesting that a knowledge society is one that is more likely to prosper economically than one that is not. Such a society is also more likely to spend part of its surplus social capital and to encourage the well-off in its population to also commit some of their disposable income to sponsoring a life of the mind; allocating resources to researchers to enable them to buy the leisure that is a necessary ingredient for a true engagement in knowledge production. The upshot is that those societies that are dedicated to the expansion of the frontiers of knowledge are often the same societies with more robust economies and those that are not, in the name of sponsoring only or largely that knowledge that promotes immediate relevance to practical everyday concerns, lag behind.

Nothing in what I have said so far is meant to suggest that no knowledge production takes place in our various societies or that many of the pursuits that I listed in the preceding paragraphs may not be found in them. I am simply contending that, on balance, the business of valuing knowledge because it is knowledge is not the principal motivation for producing knowledge and although the associated activities do take place, they occur episodically and in enclaves; they are never so integral to our societies that they occur routinely.

For evidence of the parlous state of affairs in the area of knowledge production all one need do is look at what goes on in the knowledge industry in Africa. Just like what happens in other areas of African life, African exertions on behalf of knowledge are afflicted with a terminal case of extraversion. All or most work that is done locally is not done for immediate or direct local consumption. Rather they are denominated by whether or not they would be good enough for inclusion in overseas outlets. Universities routinely insist that for advancement, their faculty should publish an overwhelming percentage of their intellectual production in so-called "international journals." Let us for a moment ignore the fact that an international journal is always a local journal where it is located, especially given that in the arts and social sciences, the bulk of the materials that such journals publish are designed to enhance, in the first instance, local conversations. That is why those journals always have a preponderance of local authors writing on issues of local interests. Let us also set aside, even as we acknowledge, the importance of scholars talking to and with one another across geographical or cultural boundaries for the sake of pushing back the frontiers of knowledge. And there can be no doubt that African societies are not alone in expecting this of their scholars and researchers. But I think that this practice is inimical to genuine knowledge production of the type that is characteristic of knowledge societies.

In the first place, the idea that outsiders are better judges of the quality of our intellectual output is an oblique acknowledgment that we are either incapable of creating or unwilling to create local quality control mechanisms that would make our local journals and other outlets sources that the rest of the world would want to consult when they seek knowledge produced in our neck of the woods. Journals require referees and readers for their dialectic to be completed. Peer review mechanisms are requisite. In local knowledge, local experts should be interested in furthering knowledge. Our countries lack the required community. When we had resources, we did not create them. This means that it is not appropriate to blame their current lack on inadequate resources.

Secondly, we are almost saying that our scholars can be good only when they have been so certified by outsiders. We may not see it this way but this manner of proceeding is a collective confession of our lack of confidence in our own abilities, practices, processes, and institutions. We are confessing that we do not trust our own judgment of quality. This is ironic coming from people who have made a fetish, at least at the rhetorical level, of doing their thing in their own way, the principal reason for widespread African opposition to modernity. Thus work that is designed to contribute to local knowledge is never directly offered to its consumers; it is only indirectly so. An implication of this manner of proceeding is that the primary motivation for doing the work is not the production of knowledge but the garnering of honorifics from outsiders.

Such work as is disseminated outside becomes part of the mode of knowledge production of the host country and only indirectly part of ours. Think of it this way. During the period that I finished my doctoral work in Canada, about eight other Nigerians submitted dissertations to the same school. We were not the only ones. There were Ghanaians, Tanzanians, and Sudanese among us. As far as I know, for all of us Africans, we stopped talking with one another once we left Canada. So, we no longer shared our work on Africa with one another but with outsider others who continued to be enriched by our production while we are steadily impoverished. The result: any student attending my alma mater would have access to the foundational outputs of nine Nigerian scholars, not to talk of those of the other Africans. And because Canada is a knowledge society, all dissertations defended in the country are deposited in the National Library in the nation's capital. The Nigerian student has access to none or at most one or, in the unlikely instance of having two of us teaching at the same school, two of the dissertations. Given that more than half of the dissertations involved dealt with Nigerian themes, the reader can begin to see how the fact that the foundational works of our careers end up being a part of another's knowledge repertory is solid evidence for the absence of a knowledge society in Nigeria. Our products become part of Canada's depository: Nigeria has no depository to speak of. The absence of local journals and publishing means that we could no longer argue with one another in settings that promote wide dissemination and the involvement of many contributors.

What I have just said applies with equal force to the repeated required alienation of our knowledge products to outside outlets. The consequences are more deleterious in the sphere of the cultural sciences. One must doubt the commitment of those who insist that results of research carried out at home on local themes should be published outside to be recognised. In the first place, given that the readers for the external journals are unlikely to have the requisite expertise or fluency in the idiom in which the research was conducted and reported, the quality of recognition must remain suspect. Secondly, the audience for the published results must be small indeed given that the overwhelming audience that can judge rightly of the true merits of the research is at home. If there is a genuine interest in contributing to and enhancing discourse, the primary target audience must be the local one.

To take one example, when Indians inaugurated subaltern discourse, the founding publications were locally sourced, and much of it was Indians talking to and fighting it out with one another. Doubtless, the quality of the contributions eventually attracted the world to them and the rest, as they say, is history. Had Indian scholars been compelled to strive for overseas recognition, there might have been no takers for what they were interested in talking about; or their overseas editors and referees might have coerced them into changing their language to fit the styles and patterns of such journals and the discourses that they were interested in.

Very few people now evince any awareness that the debates inaugurated by Ngugi wa Thiong'o and his interlocutors at the University of Nairobi in the mid 1970s, regarding the identity and scope of the then department of English at the university and its later spread to Nigeria and other places rightly form part of the genesis of what is now called Postcolonial Studies. The reason is not far to seek. Indians have a record of their debates in the journals that they chartered which have continued to publish; the African journals are all extinct. Finally, because African knowledge production is extraverted, the direction of research, and the choice of themes and methodologies are not driven by considerations of what would enable the best self-knowledge or the thorough investigation of local phenomena but by whether or not foreign sponsors—from foundations to journal editors to prospective consumers—would be interested in the research agenda.

From the foregoing, we can now see why the kinds of robust activities that normally mark a vibrant autochthonous mode of knowledge production are not much evident in the African continent. For the most part, African research programmes seem to be appendages to other peoples', other traditions', central concerns. What should have been the primary concern of indigenous modes of knowledge production—making sense of the world primarily through the lenses of our own history and idioms, borrowing as and when necessary but always domesticating, making our own what is borrowed—is relegated to inferior status and what should have been peripheral is elevated to the core of our scholarly interventions. No one should be surprised that few in the world look to Africa for insights that might be garnered from our strivings for insights into the human condition and its fate in a hostile and fragile world. This, ultimately, is why African universities do not make it onto any lists of the world's best and are unlikely to in the near future.

It is partly why exile—internal and external—is always the first option for African academics. What does exile mean? There are many modes of enacting exile. Many people mistakenly believe that only those of us who have emigrated physically are in exile. In this discussion, exile does not mean exit from the physical territory where one once plied one's trade. It refers instead to the world of knowledge production. Some of us who are physically removed have continued to work in knowledge production tied to Africa, not just in the themes, but also in where we place the results of our research. Yet there are others who are in both physical and intellectual exile. Then there are the internal exiles who, though they remain on the soil, have abandoned knowledge production for greener pastures in government, university administration, politics, or industry.

When I say that exile is the first option, I mean that it is almost as if African academics look at knowledge production as preparatory to other stations in life. Being an academic is never enough. I remember a professor at a Nigerian university who, on being promoted full professor, announced to some of us that he hoped he could make it now that he had become a full professor. His musing was instructive. Unbeknownst to him, he spoke the mind of many in African academia. It is why being professor is never enough: they have to be chair of their departments, dean of faculty, deputy vice chancellor, vice chancellor, with absolutely no mind being paid to their suitability for those positions both in terms of their skill sets or their temperaments. Moving into those positions has become almost like assuming a hereditary chieftaincy with each looking to take his or her turn at the lever of power. Were knowledge production the primary focus, many of those positions would be at best needless distractions or, at worst, career destroyers that threaten to retard one's research, divert one away from the excitement of making discoveries, etc. They would, in the most, be filled by people, including academics, better suited for them to the benefit of everyone involved.

That ours are not knowledge societies is why it has become increasingly difficult to source young brilliant minds for recruitment into the ranks of budding workers in the vineyards of knowledge in various African countries. It is why it is easier for African scholars to obtain funding from outside to study their own reality than it is for them to do so from internal sources. It is why the publishing industry has collapsed and disappeared from much of the continent. It is why many African cultures, including some of the most intellectually and materially advanced, are staring precipitous decline and eventual extinction in the face. I am not being an alarmist. I base these conclusions on some of the concerns that are being expressed daily in numerous media outlets and academic fora across the continent.

It should by now be clear what we need to do to rectify the shortcomings that I have identified in the preceding pages. Modern society prides itself on being a knowledge society. The foundation of this orientation is located in that tenet of modernity respecting the centrality of Reason. Yes, I know all the criticisms that have been and can be levelled at what is usually dismissed by critics as logocentrism. Nor do I want to underplay the unhappy history of where philosophers assigned Africans in the human chain on account of their denial of our possessing Reason. The irony is that in the current situation in various African countries where we are urging our

youth more and more to embrace "industrial and technical education" and learn useful trades, we are confirming
the racial supremacist insistence that we must forever be
hewers of wood and drawers of water in the global intellectual order. Think of it, how did a Korean university attract to their faculty a French writer who lived part of his
childhood in Nigeria, memorialised it in his writing and
went on to win the Nobel prize for literature and no Nigerian university has any relationship with him? I guess
they cannot see what "problem" would be solved by cultivating a foreign writer in a foreign tongue. In a sense,
racial supremacists need not worry: we are all too happy
now to inhabit the box of backwardness that they used to
need to shove us forcefully into. It is a mistake to shun
modernity and its associated principle of the centrality
of Reason on that score and, instead, take refuge in our
being the opposite of "Western man" driven, as we are,
if some of our thinkers are to be believed, by our being
one with the world, refusing to embrace the subject-ob-
ject distinction and apprehending the world by emotion
through participation.

I am neither deterred by the racist narratives of
modernity's principal thinkers nor persuaded by those
who accept the metaphysics of difference when it comes
to Africans' relations to the rest of humanity. Humanity
is one and Reason is no exclusive preserve of any one part
of the human family. That is, Reason is not cultural; it
does not speak one language or deploy a unique idiom. It
is there in all humanity to be deployed as each people see

fit. But the centrality that modernity endowed it with is an idiom that Africans refuse to embrace and deploy in their lives at their own peril. In this I am merely following the lead of those Africans in the nineteenth century who, barely removed from the degradation of slavery, asserted with confidence their common membership of humanity and set about, with a little education by their mentors, creating revolutionary social experiments designed to remake their societies in the modern image. They were the genuine revolutionaries whose ambitions were thwarted when the administrator class became the principal architects and builders of formal colonialism.

Our forebears took seriously the idea of the centrality of Reason and rebuked their tutors for not being consistent in their professions. They quickly saw through the contradiction inherent in, on one hand, proclaiming the unity of humanity and, on the other, denying a group of humans their membership of the species. That is, unlike us at the present time, they were not ready to concede the exclusive ownership of Reason to any one group of humans. They went to school; they became scientists, poets, theologians, philologists, ethnographers, medical researchers, and so on. They did not think that their intellectual strivings should be denominated by the requirement to solve practical problems. In other words, they were committed to the creation of knowledge societies. They thought up schemes for universities to be modelled on the centres of learning for which Africa was once famous: they recalled the glory that were Egypt and Mali, Ethiopia, and Meroe-Kush.

These were the lofty ambitions that were thwarted by colonialism. What colonialism did instead was to midwife an education system that was shorn of any high ideals but suffused with crass instrumentalism: produce personnel who would keep the colonial bureaucracy and the limited commercial life designed for Africans rolling. The manpower development and nation-building motif was born of that "perfumed abortion."

Unfortunately, after independence, precisely because the education system crafted by colonialism did not set out to construct knowledge societies—they were set up deliberately to subvert knowledge—Africans who insisted on the centrality of Reason were branded rebels, radicals, etc., who indulged in sedition, insubordination towards constituted authority, and generally preached the overthrow of the old order jointly made up of renegade chiefs and retrograde colonial administrators. This stigmatisation of Reason has been deepened by those who succeeded to power in the post-independence period, and they have never sought to critically scrutinise the colonial legacy and get rid of it. It is perhaps a mark of how successfully colonialism underdeveloped African Reason that it is yet to recover more than a half-century after so-called independence was granted the bulk of African countries.

It is time to reaffirm the centrality of Reason as the philosophical foundation for the incorporation of the society of knowledge and set about having this reflected in even the most pedestrian aspects of African life. Without doubt, the task is a lot more difficult now than at any other time in our history given the rampaging onslaught of ignorance, superstition, and any number of fundamentalisms afflicting the continent at the present time. We need to embrace the scientific orientation and, even as we may believe in the insufficiency of our nature that makes us hanker after religion or spiritual solace, we must commit to the experimental method, the firm conviction that, using reason, we can force nature to yield her innermost secrets to our probing, and that knowledge is power.

To do the above we must undo the legacy of colonialism which, in the words of its arch-philosopher, Frederick Lugard, insisted that Africans were not worthy or capable of benefitting from the "education of the intellect" but only from "character education." So Religion was an important subject and Science was not. The racist policy of excluding us from the ranks of common humanity or, when included, designating us as so primitive that we could not benefit from being exposed to or challenged by the abstract truths of modernity meant that knowledge production never aimed for any heights beyond what was considered commensurate with the primitive stage of development where we were supposed to be: subsistence agriculture; limited literacy and numeracy skills for a race whose members are destined for near permanent prostracy in the human scheme; no practice at modern government, and so on.

Not for us an education of the intellect designed to plumb the depths of nature in all its ramifications to discover fresh insights into how things work; not for us the cultivation of reason and celebration of the wonders that it has wrought; not for us the freeing up of our imagination to roam wherever its fancies may guide it in quest of the most wholesome templates for being human, the best life for humans and the most effective means for attaining same. It is in this quest that the human mind comes up with recondite ideas respecting political governance, social living, and ethics. By shutting our best minds from engagement with these kinds of issues, colonial education almost permanently stunted our intellectual evolution and rendered us forever prancing around with our minds riveted on everyday problems of survival. The preoccupation with so-called practical problems, the discouragement of knowledge production that aims to understand planets beyond our own, is the unfortunate harvest of a racist sowing that was so thorough we ourselves have never subjected it to withering scrutiny. And scrutinise it we must if we are to uproot it from our soil and join the race for uplift for us, our progeny, and just common humanity.

Africa is not lacking in the seed personnel for this transformation. As in all situations of progress, it does not require large numbers to move things forward. But it does require the kind of leadership that has the fortitude to realise that the path that the continent is on right now will only make us permanent research assistants to the rest of professional humanity. Such leadership will have to be supported and advised by intellectuals equipped with the right kind of fierce pride and confidence in their abilities, the kind of self-respect that Africans seem to lack at all levels at the present time, and an imagination that refuses to be pinned down to problems of the day but frees itself to anticipate problems that have not even presented themselves. Finally, all this will have to take place within a mode of knowledge production that is primarily "for us, by us, about us, and near us." It will be driven by awareness that, on balance, a knowledge society is its own reward.

Four

Count, Measure, and Count Again

In other words, at the commencement of the second decade of the twenty-first century, the government of the Federal Republic of Nigeria and its constituent federated states do not know roughly how many people inhabit their physical space or how that population is distributed among the units.

IN THE previous chapter, I made the case for knowledge and for pursuing it for its own sake. Certainly, some who are inclined to be mischievous may have read the case as one whose author does not care a hoot for the application of the knowledge so produced or even for any type of applied knowledge. The more charitable, maybe even sympathetic, reader would have paid attention to the other half of the title that references the rewards of creating a knowledge society. In this chapter, I spell out one kind of knowledge, and I discuss at length how pursuing it will help our societies be immeasurably better than they are at the moment. I am referring to the importance of counting and the bounteous harvest that we as a people stand to reap from a full, unabashed engagement in and with it.

Many African societies that never developed writing were not bereft of counting systems. A few of them were even home to other types of mathematical or proto-mathematical traditions. Why am I alluding to this in the present discussion? For a very simple reason: at the present time, Africans can't and, if they can, don't count or measure enough, if at all, in an age in which counting and measuring are not merely important; they are critical to life in the modern age. Not only do we live with counting and measuring in our time, they indeed circumscribe all areas of daily life as people lead it in those places where the modern model predominates. This is the fact that modern society lives or dies by counting, measuring, and counting, *ad nauseam*. It counts when it is necessary. It counts when it is utterly unnecessary. It counts for specific purposes. It counts when there is no purpose to be served. It just counts, period. And the same goes for measuring.

All of us who live in the modern heartland like the United States, to take but one example, know how crucial counting and measuring are to everyday life. Korea is an even more fascinating example. The same goes for Japan. Korea compared itself to Europe, found itself wanting, and decided to alter the imbalance. They sought to redress the imbalance between them and the West in the *indicia* of well doing. We are reminded daily of the centrality of counting in the modern age in the interminable lists that festoon modern societies' magazines, television shows, newspapers, radio advertisements, jingles, and so on. We are daily bombarded with reminders of recommended daily values of vitamin supplements, percentage intake of nutrients in food items, food pyramids, and what percentage of fruit juices is actually derived from fruit. It wasn't so long ago when we were being advised that we needed to drink so many ounces of water per day to maintain a healthy balance of liquids in our bodies.

Beyond the mundane details of food and drink, one cannot overstress the importance of counting, measuring, and calculations in various industries. Take the pharmaceutical industry, for instance. There is a direct connection between the dosage of a drug and its capacity to cure or kill you. Absent measurement, dosage becomes a hit or miss affair with all the deleterious consequences such a situation portends. For some of the most serious diseases that afflict humans, the most potent drugs require dosage measurements to the nearest decimal; otherwise the side effects of the drugs alone can destroy the patient, not to mention the risk of overdosing on them.

What I have just said does not even begin to scratch the surface of the importance of counting and measuring in the pharmaceutical industry. There are different media through which drugs are presented to the consumer. I am ignoring for the moment the battery of specialities in counting and measuring that the discipline of pharmacy and its numerous subdisciplines depend upon for their work to proceed with any promise of success. Whether a drug is presented in tablet, capsule, caplet—all solid—form; or as a suspension or syrup—all liquid form; or as a gel, cream, ointment; or as an injection or something to be intravenously administered is, to be sure, inseparable from the consideration of whether its active and inert ingredients can be accommodated for dosage in any of the forms just identified. It may be the case, in some instances, that to present the drug concerned in tablet form will require that the patient take so many tablets at once that such dosage will be impractical; or no single tablet can accommodate sufficient amounts of the relevant ingredients to make it workable. Beyond the manufacture and presentation of the drug lies the matter of its packaging. I am sure the reader can fill in the blank spaces regarding how much counting and measuring are involved there too. And in talking about the operation of the drugs, counting and measuring are no less important. A blood thinner must not do its work so well that the blood becomes too thin. What is required to dilate pupils must not leave the patient's eyes permanently altered. There is a delicate understanding of how long the effect must last so as not to cause damage or even extended inconvenience to the patient. Talk of the importance of measuring.

Take the freight industry, for another instance. The containers that are used to transport the goods that are interchanged between one part of the globe and another are so standardised in their specifications that they easily transit from the ship to port to rail and road delivery vehicles. Such is the impact of this instance of standardisation and the seamless ways in which the lowly container is integrated into the global freight industry that the BBC followed the trails of one container as it made its way from one port to another over the course of a year in 2007; a journey that saw it roll on and off in various ports in Europe, Asia, and North America. Certainly African countries are a vital part of this global freight industry, and I know that Ethiopia has a big domestic industry fabricating them. I am not sure, though, that the mindset that they symbolise in their stark simplicity and efficiency strikes a chord with us in Africa. But it is a testament to measuring and counting.

So are other areas of the transportation industry. From railroad gauges to the dimensions of rivets for various machines to tyre sizes and the angles at which the side rearview mirrors on cars are fixed, they all testify to the centrality of measuring. I have chosen two arbitrary examples. Others are sure to come up in the course of the present discussion. We do not need to multiply examples. Think rivets; electric sockets; A4 paper. The point is that it would be rare to call a society modern that does not embrace the importance of counting, measuring, and calculating.

No doubt there is a widespread diffusion of counting and mathematical systems across the African continent. Africans have been great mathematicians and used to march in tandem with the rest of humanity on that road. And there are many Africans in our own time who are in the top ranks of mathematicians and other pliers of the counting and measuring disciplines in our world. But, in spite of this historical and contemporary reality, it would be far fetched to call any of our societies a counting, measuring, and calculating society. This invites comment because even in my corner of the continent this inattention to counting and measuring has not always been the case.

As a child growing up in Ibadan, Nigeria, I recall that *púrúñtù*—illiterate people—used to distinguish between themselves and the "been-tos"—the literate ones—in terms precisely of the measuring, counting, and calculating ways of the latter. *Púrúñtù* used to deride the been-tos' penchant for measuring how many cups of rice to cook both for their families and when they entertained; for estimating to the nearest penny what specific engagements might cost, and so on. It didn't make sense to my young mind back then and, no doubt, given the cultural milieu in which I grew up, it would have been a surprise had it made sense. But looking back now, it makes a lot of sense to measure. In fact, it is a confirmation of the centrality of counting to the culture that the been-tos had been socialised into and had embraced.

The family form dominant among them or to which many of them pretended to aspire was the nuclear family. There was no extended family that roomed with them or lived in their immediate vicinity. If they had children, they were likely to be few. Cooking more than would be consumed by the family would be to risk waste. Frugality was another element of the culture they had embraced. Since only the nuclear family occupied the house, there was no possibility of other children in the compound showing up or being called upon to deal with the leftovers. Making excess food meant throwing away a part of the fixed income the family had to live on. So, consumption was adjusted to earning level and calibrated to the multiplex needs of the family. So, in a sense, the motivating idea was: Waste not, want not. Unfortunately, this investment in counting and measuring never became diffused in the larger communities, and one has reason to suspect that even among the ranks of the been-tos the commitment to counting has waned considerably, if it has not completely petered out.

Nigeria is the poster child for the inability of contemporary Africans to take counting seriously. As we write this, the country has never run a successful, accurate census. In other words, at the commencement of the second decade of the twenty-first century, the government of the Federal Republic of Nigeria and its constituent federated states do not know roughly how many people inhabit their physical space or how that population is distributed among the units. They, by extension, do not have a fair rendering of the sectoral distribution of their population in terms of occupations, age, religious affiliations, educational attainments, national identities, languages, literacy and illiteracy patterns, levels of consumption, leisure preferences, and so on. It can get even worse. I remember several years ago when we found out that a university, yes, university, did not have a firm figure of how many students it had! Three different administrative divisions of the institution offered three different figures. Of course, this is not to say that Nigeria is typical of all African countries. I have only used the example of Nigeria to illustrate how skewed our understanding of the demographic situation of the continent is when its most populous country does not know how many people live within its borders. By extension, our repeated proclamation of the continent's population and especially what percentage of that is made up of Nigerians must remain suspect.

Several implications follow from the above example. Let us explore a few of them. Given that in the global imaginary Africa is one with its maladies, it is not an accident that counting heads in the AIDS epidemic in the continent is a global obsession—"percentage of Africans living with AIDS," "percentage of every country's population living with HIV/AIDS," "percentage of world sufferers living with AIDS who live in Africa"— the list continues. We are assailed daily with figures of varying degrees of accuracy of Africa's star role in the global AIDS pandemic; a role that it seems Africans and their leaders are all too willing to assume, perhaps revel in. But if Africa's most populous nation does not know how many people inhabit its borders, how can we be sure that its sectoral breakdowns, including its AIDS-suffering component, are reliable? By the same token, given that the United Nations and other international agencies do not conduct their own census and depend instead on extrapolations and projections, we can also ask how reliable those numbers are that they are forever trotting out in respect of Africa's maladies or their magnitudes.

Let us leave aside for a moment the problem with external agencies and their AIDS statistics in Africa. Of greater importance is the fact that, given our inability to count or our unwillingness to take counting seriously, within various African countries and on the continental level, we are not in a position to know how many of our people are infected; how many have progressed to full-blown AIDS; which groups are most at risk; and why some may be more at risk than others. We need to have a fairly stable idea of the sectoral distribution of the HIV-AIDS-infected population. This is important for several reasons. For example, if we don't know how many children are infected and what the breakdown is of their age brackets, we will not be in a position to estimate the cost of managing their lives with the virus: retroviral drugs, psychological and other social help, how or whether they will be productive members of society as they grow up, and so on. I have singled out HIV-AIDS in part because it is where the money has been in recent years for research and attention.

It is clear that HIV-AIDS is not the most devastating of the afflictions that stalk Africa and its peoples. Malaria takes that accursed prize. Yet few are the initiatives within the African continent to eradicate this scourge. Relevant to the present discussion is the absence of serious counting of the consequences of malaria across the continent and measuring of its impact on productivity. I don't want to believe that these are not concerns that Africans have. But I think a good part of the reason why they are not the object of widespread attention is the palpable lack of an accounting of their impact beyond the experiential level of its victims and the politicians who wish to rub shoulders with Bill Gates when he comes to give money for malaria research.

Let me use an analogy to illustrate the pitfalls of not counting costs. Greeting and exchanging pleasantries are a very critical measure of sophistication and civility in Yorùbá culture. Some might even suggest that it is a measure of an individual's very humanity. I doubt that there are many of us who belong to that culture who have ever bothered to consider the costs—that is, count the costs—of greeting and exchanging pleasantries. I know this because at various times in the past when I have pointed out how inefficient our pattern of giving and receiving courtesy is, my compatriots indicated to me how little attention they had paid to the issue. They have never bothered to count the costs of greeting. But the practice is not without costs.

How is this so? To greet another in Yorùbá with a "hi" equivalent is to insult that person. Okay, let's say you deploy instead the multi-syllabic, two-word standard, "Good morning," that is only slightly less offensive. The culture prizes asking after the family, the household, remark if the people involved have not seen each other in days, and so on. Now even if you left your home early enough to commute to work on time, by the time you "greet properly" all who desire to show you their well wishes for one single morning, you may well find yourself scrambling to make it to work on time. The key phrase here is "on time." Because we do not place much premium on "man-hours" lost and the production that is thereby preempted, these losses go unapprehended, much less lamented. I would like to suggest that in the same way that we fail to apprehend the costs of greeting, we similarly fail to count the costs of the many afflictions that occur on the continent. Bad roads, traffic jams, and absent infrastructure readily come to mind. Maybe if we counted the costs we would be less lackadaisical in our attitude towards them.

Enough, for now, of the malady-driven aspect. However important the preceding may be, I am more concerned with the deleterious results of not taking counting seriously in African countries. Take, for example, the growing efflux of Africans from rural areas to the continent's burgeoning cities. Yet, African scholars love to continue telling stories of widespread rural living and the "villageal" character of much of African life. I do not want to be misunderstood. I have nothing against villages. The problem is that those who hold Africa to be radically, possibly incommensurably, different from other humans and, by extension, other cultures, insist—and African scholars and functionaries oblige them—on a uni-dimensional rendering of the African situation. Africans and their cultures are irredeemably simple, their social organisations even more so and their social relations not much more complex than the village type. This is what makes everyone think that Africa is a continent of tribes, not nations; villages not cities; and primordial loyalties, not civic associations structured and legitimised by conventions. Unfortunately, one who thinks that the cause of the village is helped by this singular sclerotic focus is in for some serious disappointment. In exactly the same way that there is little engagement with the fortunes of cities there is little interest—beyond that of exotica and "scholarship" booty—in the vicissitudes of village life.

Two immediate consequences follow from this disconnection in the scholarly imaginary in Africa between the reality of exponentially expanding urbanisation and the continuing misplaced focus on the village as the locus of relevant knowledge of the African experience. In the first place, a lack of solid knowledge of the numbers of people moving back and forth in the continent between urban and rural settings and all other points in-between means that people move into population centres whose services—housing, sewage treatment, sewer, transportation and communication, power, water, etc.—are quickly overwhelmed by new arrivals with the resulting multi-plication of slums and the ensuing degradation of both humans and their environment. I am convinced that we are too accepting of slums in our physical spaces. It is almost as if we are resigned to the inevitability of slums in our urban centres. Remember, I went looking for them in Toronto, Canada. Such an attitude, I think, bespeaks a lack of respect for ourselves, our fellows, and the physical spaces we love to call home. We reconcile to the existence of slums without betraying any anxiety as to what they represent for our sense of who we are, our humanity, and how that humanity is perceived by other humans and what it means for how they treat us and whatever else pertains to us.

I have often wondered at the source of our lack of respect for ourselves and the contempt in which we hold one another. Notice how I have put this indictment in collective terms because it is difficult to look at our physical environment, rural and urban, and come to any judgment other than that we, as a people, must have an extremely low opinion of ourselves and do not think that our likes are deserving of physical spaces of beauty and healthfulness. If it were the case that we build our cities and make them paragons of beauty and wholesome living while neglecting our villages, one would at least point to some level of respect for our humanity in the urban areas; and vice versa for the rural areas. The tragedy is that our cities are marked by planlessness, unspeakable ugliness and, generally, the proliferation of conditions absolutely inimical to the efflorescence of what is best about our humanity. The difference between our cities and our villages is only one of scale: we invest in ugly!

Perhaps if we paid a little more attention to counting, we might thereby apprehend the ugliness that results from unplanned cities, unanticipated explosions in populations, nonexistent infrastructure, and so on. These are all interrelated phenomena. Or maybe if we had more respect for ourselves and our fellow citizens, we would have taken counting more seriously and put in place the appropriate infrastructure that would enable us to cope with the growth of our cities; even ensure that the growth is more ordered. One of the reasons that the rural areas are emptying so quickly and small to medium-sized cities are losing more and more of their population to the big cities has to do with the dire lack of opportunities as well as the harshness of living conditions, not to mention the monotony of existence, in any location outside of the big cities. But what I am calling for here may be more difficult to achieve given what I have called our inability to count or our inattentiveness to the importance of counting. If we do not know how many we are and the different characteristics of each sector of the population, it stands to reason that we would not be in any position to know what the needs are of each specific sector of the population, how those needs change over time, and how we might go about sourcing the wherewithal for the satisfaction of those apprehended needs. These needs include jobs, food, housing, healthcare, education, and leisure services for our populace.

Of course, people migrate into the big cities in anticipation of a better life, more opportunities, and greater variety in their lives. We know that such hopes are often forlorn in our urban landscapes. What results from the unrelenting influx of new residents into our cities and the unpreparedness of the relevant authorities to accommodate them and expand services and facilities quickly enough to ensure a decent level of existence for the new migrants? It is the creation of new slums and the expansion of existing ones. It is an index of our widely diffused penchant for self-deception that the well-off among us—the money-bags, upper classes, etc.—believe that their ability to cocoon themselves in gated estates or newly-reclaimed islands of quiet, grandeur, and beauty frees them from having to deal with the ugly spectacle that daily life is for the rest of their fellow citizens. The contempt that they have for their less circumstanced fellows is obvious in the fact that they are not scandalised by the inhumane lives that their fellows lead and the utter ugliness in which those lives unfold. The irony is that their contempt for their compatriots is matched by their own very deep, even if unacknowledged, lack of self-respect.

I would like to tell a story and relate an anecdote to illustrate the lack of self-respect on the part of Africa's ruling classes. It was sometime in the mid-nineties. I was visiting Nigeria, and one evening I hitched a ride with an inter-city *kabúkabú* driver plying the route between two of Nigeria's cities. I was the only fare; business must have been very slow that day. We struck up a conversation. My driver, who looked like a mid-level civil servant—educated, well turned-out, well-spoken, and owned his own car that he had turned into an occasional cab, as was the case that evening—went on singing the praise of one of the most prominent Yorùbá monarchs; his fame, his wealth, his influence, his power, and so on. At some point, I cut in and told the driver [let's call him Mike] that I would never pray for the monarch's kind of fortune which Mike found so worthy of effusive praise and celebration. He promptly cautioned me to not curse myself. Why would I not pray to be similarly blessed, he queried. I persisted. He relented and asked me to share with him why I would not wish for similar blessings. I told him a bit about my former life in Nigeria and the city where I used to live and worked as a teacher. I let him know that as of the time of our conversation I had exiled myself and lived in the United States.

Where I lived in the United States, I proceeded to educate Mike, there were no rich people. My neighbourhood was made up of condominiums, rental apartments, and different sizes of single-family homes, none of which would qualify as "grand." Most of us who lived in my neighbourhood were professionals, graduate students, and other low to middle income workers. The stability and quality of the area were enhanced by my then employer's soft loan programme to enable its staff and faculty to purchase homes in the neighbourhood—another example of how universities are related to their locality. But the modesty of our dwellings or of the neighbourhood in which they were situated did not mean epileptic power supply to our homes, craters on our roads, dust when it was dry or having to ford gutters or wade through muddy puddles when it rained to get to our houses or businesses in our area, or open sewers that fouled up our air and posed a permanent threat of disease and pestilence for us and our families.

I then asked Mike the following questions: this monarch, with his fabulous wealth and storied connections in Nigeria and overseas, was he exempt from the ravages of irregular electricity supply? No, he answered but quickly added: the monarch has generators. I replied: I knew you would say that. Did the monarch's generator not make noise or spew out pollutants that were diffused in the air over the palace when it was operated? Yes, he said, it did. Was the monarch immune from having to shout in conversations with others in his living room over the din of generator engines? No, he said. And did the monarch have a specially adapted respiratory system that made his lungs impervious to the penetration of particulates from the generator's emissions? No, he offered. Since I knew the city very well over which this monarch presided, I asked Mike if he could describe for me what the road outside the palace gate was like. Chock full of potholes, he replied. So, I rejoined, every time the monarch set out with his convoy to go anywhere outside of his palace, he had to go through *pòtòpótó*, that is, wade through muddy puddles, and he was rocked by the impact of his chauffeur hitting or avoiding potholes. I summed up: so our glorious monarch, with all his wealth and influence, lived a poorer and more deprived life in his domain than the auto mechanic did who was my neighbour in my area of the city where I lived in the United States. This is a story that can be told of any monarch in Nigeria; the same for our moneyed classes, new and old. I asked Mike if he thought I made sense. He eased his car to a gentle stop on the curb, turned on the inside light and said: I had to stop and have some idea of who you are and what you look like. You have brought me a new awareness of why it is one thing to have money and a different thing to live well. He volunteered that he no longer thought that my sentiment amounted to or approximated a curse.

Now, the anecdote. In the city where I used to live and work before I left Nigeria, a dear friend and one-time colleague and I got together one Saturday afternoon and decided that we were going to go out and blow some good money entertaining ourselves. We wanted to splurge. We jumped in his car and proceeded to drive around the city for the next two hours looking for where to splurge. It was a fruitless engagement. After two hours of a driving merry-go-round, we settled for the same old pepper soup joint that we wanted to avoid. As a Yorùbá adage would put it: *ojú towóo wa!* We had money, but we had nothing to spend it on. Our money was shamed!

Between my encounter with Mike and the brief anecdote, something significant can be detected. What happened to my friend and me would have been the experience of any member of the so-called upper classes if they live in Ile-Ife, or any of Nigeria's major cities, with very few exceptions, even as I write this, almost a decade and a half later. In other words, if one is interested in the standard of living that is supposed to go with a certain level of income, most of our cities cannot offer it. Put simply: our middle and upper classes can't live as well as they should in our countries. Unfortunately, it appears that this point is lost on our ruling classes. Part of the explanation can be traced to the fact that they have never adverted their minds to the real cost of not having, in this instance, leisure and recreation spots in their immediate vicinity; a lack that forces them, on occasion, to drive long distances to relax. The tragedy is that, in the absence of this apprehension, our ruling classes foolishly think that they solve the problem once they can have the latest satellite or cable technology installed in their residences and make enough money to go to London or Paris or New York or, now, Dubai to sate their more "cosmopolitan" yearnings. It never occurs to them that the transaction costs of these alternatives are otherwise unbearable, maybe even scandalous.

The contempt that Africa's moneyed classes have for their less circumstanced fellows is what makes them think that their cocoons suffice to insulate them from the ugliness in which their fellows live out their desperate lives. But we have seen that this ambition is an illusion. Meanwhile, their lack of self-respect will not let them see that their lives are tethered permanently to that ugliness that they think is not theirs to set aright. What is more, all it takes is a closer look at their lives to see that, regardless of what they think of themselves, the evidence points to the fact that insofar as they fail to create the kind of tide that will lift all boats, they will have to continue to risk life and limb if they live in Oyo or Abeokuta to enjoy the pleasures of the city in Lagos and, if in Lagos, to go to Europe, the United States or, lately, Dubai, to enjoy the pleasures of modern living. When they think that their sorry lives behind barbed wires in residences that mimic opulence and manifest faux beauty, well supplied with their boreholes, industrial-strength generators, and satellite television, lift them above their compatriots, they lie. They must be the only ones who don't know it. Truth be told, they spend more time in the muck of the surrounding slums—traffic jams, potholed streets, darkness galore, foul-smelling, disease-causing, pestilence-threatening open sewers, dust, *pòtòpótó*—indeed, they spend more time in the ugliness of their cityscapes than they do in the contrived beauty of their isolated palaces!

It is time to reconnect to our theme in this chapter: counting and measuring. If we had paid attention to establishing a baseline statistic for our settlements, rural and urban, with accurate censuses, we would have been in a position to make intelligent and well-grounded projections regarding the sectoral distribution of our population, identify areas that are likely to attract new migrants, ascertain trends in the population in different parts of the country, anticipate efflux, and maybe even prevent migrations by reorienting resources—infrastructure, investment, job creation programmes, leisure services, education institutions, new industries—to areas where there are indications that opportunities are becoming scarce for that sector of the population that is usually inclined and adventurous enough to move: the youth. But if we don't even have the foggiest idea as to what percentage of our population falls within the at-risk category, how are we going to put in place the mechanisms to cope with that contingency? The slummification of our physical spaces is a symptom of failure: the failure to respect ourselves and our fellow citizens, to commit to creating humane conditions for our existence, and to work assiduously to create the material resources to ensure that no African lives in conditions that are subhuman. The results will redound to the quality of life for both the rich and the poor.

So far, we have been examining the first of two consequences that arise from the disconnection we have apprehended in the African scholarly imaginary between the exponentially expanding urbanisation of the continent and the persistent but misplaced focus on the village as the locus from where to derive relevant knowledge of African life and thought at the present time.

Let us now explore the second consequence. Because the authorities have not wised up to the importance of counting, they experience the influx of numbers as an adversity rather than an advantage. Here we come directly to the impact of not knowing how many inhabit our geopolitical spaces. Knowing roughly how many people live in, say, a city at a given point in time provides an important base line from which to plan for future population increases and expansion of services. But we should not think that numbers are important only from the standpoint of providing services.

A modern economy runs on indirect, almost invisible, taxation. Numbers, when properly harnessed, mean revenue, bankability, creditworthiness—selling bonds, attracting loans and investments—all resources that cities all around the world rely upon to make life more livable for their teeming inhabitants.

This is another one of those points that gets lost in the shuffle the importance of which can easily be demonstrated. Our polities experience numbers in one of two, both unhelpful, ways. First, we are completely unmindful of it. There is an irony here. We do strive, when we have ceremonies and festivities, to have as many people as possible attend them. So, in a sense, we see some positive value in numbers. But this is deceptive. For, just as often as we welcome numbers, we do not do a good job of estimating how many might attend, and we end up scrambling, trying to cope with what usually turns out to be larger than expected numbers. Or we cook too much and waste some of it. We welcome numbers but we do nothing to indicate that this matters. This is what I mean by our being unmindful of numbers. It happens often enough on small scales in the big social parties that we love to throw at the least prompting. It is magnified in our national lives when we are heedless of the importance of counting for policy-making and policy execution.

Secondly, we experience numbers as a negative presence or value. This is related to the first way. It is easy to see why this is the case. If we have numbers that we are not prepared for, we aggravate the people that make up those numbers. They become impatient, angry, and riotous. We ourselves are frustrated at their impatience, anger, and, on occasion, violence. It is exactly the same thing that happens with the numbers that overwhelm our urban spaces. Think of chaos in city traffic and at bus stops. Because we are not ready for them, we wish that the migrants would go back to where they came from; political leaders and opinion makers are busy exhorting people in the cities to leave them and go make a life for themselves in the less frenetic settings of rural settlements. Meanwhile, it often does not resonate with our politicians, scholars, and policy-makers that many of those same individuals would not have wended their way to the cities had there been opportunities in their hometowns or villages. Opportunities are quantifiable and the centrality of counting to tracking them need not be over-emphasised.

Now imagine that we start from a situation in which we have a fairly solid idea of the numbers to start with and that is the base we work from. That is, we know how many people live in, to take an arbitrary example, the city of Ibadan, the various productive endeavours they are involved in, the levels of income they have, and the volume of economic activities that occur in the city. When you have these numbers and you are in the city of Ibadan, things must look good because you have what is at the base of most cities' prosperity: large populations. We can now see what qualitative difference counting makes. As I write this, Ibadan and the rest of our misbegotten cities experience numbers as a burden. But if those who run them were to realise that numbers are a source of strength: huge revenues, the possibility of being able to raise funds on the capital markets, both at home and abroad, creditworthiness, and so on, their attitudes will change. This is the only condition in which local government will have real meaning, and the current dependence on the whims of those who run the state and federal governments as well as, in the Nigerian case, on the fortunes of oil on the world market, will reduce if not disappear completely. Outside of these forms of revenue, there are numerous other possibilities, for example, sales tax on goods and services in the city. Levying this tax requires, yet again, paying attention to who sells and who buys what in the city and putting in place the mechanism for assessment and collection.

How well our cities, and by extension our states, fare in these activities will depend on how efficiently they exploit their tax base, the size of which counting will reveal to them. Managing the revenues they raise will be evidence for those from whom they seek to raise more capital for infrastructural projects, improvement of social services, constructing institutions for leisure like art galleries and museums, stadia, and so on. The construction of such facilities and the expansion of access to services for current residents of the city concerned will likely attract to the city new residents who are looking for better lives for themselves and their progeny, and this will, in turn, expand the city's tax base. Those that the city approaches to invest in it by lending it money or buying its municipal bonds will, as a result of the kind of performance I just described, be persuaded that the city offers a possible good return on the investment that they make when they buy the city's securities.

What do cities need to take advantage of the strengths that I have been describing? First, a city needs a modern bureaucracy: civil servants who are insulated from politics, who are chosen not based on who their godfathers are (about which see the next chapter) or whether or not we can identify their genetic roots in the city, but on merit anchored on their talents and expertise, who identify with the city and express their civic pride by how tight a ship they run and how well the citizens are looked after, thanks to their work. Beyond the bureaucracy, the city needs a solid bank of professionals; no, they don't have to be in the city's employ, but they sure have to be in the city. These will include economists, public finance experts, statisticians, actuarians, financial planners, and others in the counting professions. To start with, many of these experts will already make the financial fortunes of the city part of their daily concerns in their line of work because they are probably looking for value investments for their employers, and a city of more than a million people is quite a market to hit for profitable engagements. No doubt some of the last category of workers will be in the city's employ but, in addition, the city will need rational accounting systems, budget units suffused with experts in money management, expenditure control, human resource managers who are able to design and manage the consumption of human and material resources and who have charge of monitoring where the money goes, how well or ill it is spent as well as whether or not the personnel employed delivers value for money, and so on.

Counting enables us to make estimates of who uses city facilities, how often, and with what intensity. Many of these facilities have life spans, weight limits, climate issues, and so on. Think of it, we have no idea how many vehicles ply our roads and what kinds they are: cars, trucks, trailers, buses, buggies, bicycles, mopeds, and so on. Nor do we know who or what they carry, in what numbers and what the relative weights of their freights are. We build the roads anyway using figures that we conjure, if that! More often than not, we build roads because we want to award contracts and get our cuts! Even when we build them for service, because we cannot or will not count, the roads are not built in ways that they might last. We pluck an imaginary number, say, 10,000 cars using the road per day with each bearing an assumed tonnage, and so on. We project that with that level of usage the materials used and the design employed will bear wear and tear inflicted by that number of users for ten years before it will need a serious upgrade or reconstruction. Even if we used the best materials and design, if 20,000 cars a day end up using the road soon after construction, assuming that we were right about the tonnage, it is obvious that the road's life span will be cut in half to 5 years. I have kept it simple. If you assume that passenger cars would each routinely carry the allotted five passengers that they are designed for, it is obvious that you don't know Africa. And I am ignoring for the moment the widespread non-interest in maintenance of our infrastructure. For failure to take numbers seriously and crunch them properly before we put the road together, what we have is a road that might not even last the shortened span if, for instance, it were to fall victim to some severe weather-related emergency. That is, the severe intensity of use may not be the only problem. We do not have in many of our countries knowledge of our soils; so it is unlikely that the building of that road was based on any solid knowledge of the soil formation all along the length of the road. We should not even talk of anticipating weather patterns: we don't have accumulated records of our weather history.

Again, we have shown how simple counting and measuring enable us to make projections regarding future usage of our facilities, services, and institutions, and calculations of what will be needed to meet those future contingencies. We can multiply what we just said for other sectors of our lives. In the area of health services, for another instance, we need to know the number of doctors, the ratio of doctors to patients; the same for other health care professionals. When, as is the case in most African countries, the doctor/patient ratio is too high, it is to be expected that there will be disutilities to both doctors—overworking, burnout, exodus from the system—and patients—dismal quality of care. And it is not enough to have doctors. In Europe and North America, there is a high demand for nurses in all categories because everyone knows that doctors alone cannot run the health care delivery system. Doctors and ancillary professionals are required more in a situation where preventive services are not well developed. Crucial to the development of effective preventive services is the development of the fields of epidemiology and public health, two sure areas of the health system that are dominated by counting. It is where we figure out what is the cause and distribution of what ails us; what kills us; what changes we need to make in our environment—physical and social—that might enable us to minimise the play of such causative agents in our collective lives.

The pay-off from taking counting seriously extends far beyond cities raising revenue and providing services. The fact of the matter is that counting pays. This is where we can see the tight connection between knowledge and what we have been talking about. The graduates of our universities whose knowledge base has been broadened, whose imagination has been trained, who are imbued with a sense of the possible, and who are generally fired with appropriate pride in their heritage, will be ready to go into these different areas acquiring the relevant skills along the way and perform wonders for the lowliest of our peoples. Having been schooled in the ways of the humanities, they are less likely to be detached from the fate of those in the slums that we talked about earlier, and they will not be satisfied with merely individualising solutions to systemic and collective problems.

Think of the number of young mathematics and statistics graduates who will be employed to gather, collate, and analyse the numbers that would need to be collected. Think of the army of actuarians, adjusters, consultants, and ancillary professionals to be recruited from the ranks of graduates of physics, sociology, religious studies, or music that will help cities and small towns alike, not to talk of states, set up models and calibrate data to reach the optimum results from their outlays. Nor should I omit to mention the battery of professionals—engineers of all descriptions, masons, bricklayers, janitors, project managers, quantity surveyors, mortgage brokers, bankers—that would be required to execute the huge public works that Africa's cities need to make them livable in the twenty-first century. These are the people who would work on the power grid and how to expand it; the transportation network and movement and distribution of people; birth and death rates; marriage rates; the sectoral distribution of old and young, productive and nonproductive; tracking the production of goods and services; making future projections of food, education, transportation, communication, healthcare, water, energy needs both long and short term; personnel for them: how many jobs to be created and at what rate to take account of natural progression in birth and maturation rates; calorie intake for children; export possibilities, and, above all, fabricating a modern economy.

Unfortunately, because African intellectuals never see possibilities, only adversity, in numbers and few African leaders dare dream big for their people and countries, what we have been talking about does not show up on their radar screens. What is more, they would be easily dismissed as impossible dreams. It should be obvious by now that if I ever, even for a fleeting moment, thought that all that I have been canvassing would have to depend even if minimally on the aid budgets of the rest of the world for Africa, I would have to be stark, raving mad to make the case.

There are so many ways in which the fortunes of the continent and its peoples can be improved by counting, measuring, and calculating. I doubt that too many people will deny the crucial role of rational street numbering systems in a credit-driven economy. As banal as it sounds, having a record of previous residences and being able to piece together the elements of the prospective credit applicant's life cannot be overemphasised. One can say the same for the simple business of renting residences. The simple task of registering births is not so simple once one begins to work through the consequences that attach to the simple fact of having a new addition, not just to the immediate family of which the new bundle of joy is a putative member, but to the larger community of fellow citizens, with whom she will live the better part of her life and many of whom will contribute, even if indirectly, to her upbringing and to the general business of socialising her into productive membership of their society. Again, a communalist orientation does not avail in these endeavours.

Don't let us limit our purview to the singular birth. Let us talk instead of all the children that are born in a single year in a given slice of a complex society, say, a state within Nigeria or a region in Ghana or province in Kenya. In the first place, we need a starting point to track their journeys through life beginning with the sheer fact of how many of them live to see their first birthdays and subsequent ones. If the numbers indicate that quite a number of them do not live to see their first birthdays, we quickly know that we have a problem, and we set in motion the processes that will enable us to get to the root of the problem. If the indicators are that a lot of them are living up to school age, a society that is desirous of ensuring a good life for its members has to worry about and make provisions for the education of the children involved—preschool, kindergarten, primary school, to begin with. Hence, projections will have to be made for how many school spaces would be needed; how many teachers, teachers' helpers, janitors, nutritionists, and so on would be required to ensure that the children have the best facilities possible. Add to these the panoply of school supplies, building requirements, and you have tremendous possibilities for job creation that is bound to occupy the energies of many of the parents of the children concerned, even as the success of such engagements will ensure that future jobs for the children will be there when they grow up. They will need, as do current adults and others in the community, power, water, sewer, healthcare, educational, leisure, and sundry other facilities including, but not limited to, increasing road, rail, and other transportation and communication services. Given these conditions it is obvious that the amount of counting that needs to be done becomes prodigious.

But we cannot stop there, either. In part because we do not pay heed to the centrality of counting which, if we did, would challenge us to think more expansively in terms of how to make our resources yield maximum returns for our welfare, many items that we ordinarily do not act as if we realise their importance will enjoy the attention that they deserve both for their own sake and for ours. Africa's forests are disappearing at an alarming rate. It is bad enough that they, especially old forests, are being logged to extinction. It is worse that this is all happening in the absence of any serious census of our natural resources: how many species of plants and animals inhabit our boundaries and how many we are losing to human activities over which we can exercise some control and how many we are losing to attrition, that is, the normal evolution of nature. How is the environment going to be affected by the loss of particular plant and animal species, and what implications might all these have for our future prosperity and health? Given what I said in the previous chapter, we probably think there is no point to this kind of counting since there are no obvious practical problems to be solved by so doing.

Does anybody know the oldest soccer club in Africa? When the first soccer match was played in the continent? Where? Who scored the first goal? Who is the player who has scored the most goals in continental, local, regional, national, or club competitions? Or the one who has the most caps for appearing in his country's colours? Or the youngest to have scored a goal in league or any other significant competition? Or Africa's no. 1 referee? Or the longest serving or one who has refereed the most games? Who are Africa's top athletes? Which is the longest continuous street in Africa? How many Ph.D.s does any given African country produce in any given year? Are some degrees in some areas more needed than others? How are those degrees distributed among the different disciplines? How many Ph.D.s does a country have? How many will it need in how many disciplines in how many years? What is the volume of fresh water consumed every day, week, month, or year by a given country or state or city or region? How much fresh water is available? How long is the supply projected to last and at what rate of consumption? How many polio, tetanus, or diphtheria vaccines will be needed for what complement of a given population in a given year? How many more might be needed over the long haul? What percentage of children in any given area suffer from malnutrition? What is the severity of malnutrition in any given cohort of the population's children? How many children are born out of wedlock? How many children are born to single-female-headed households? How much water is there in various bodies of water that dominate the African landscape? The number of clothes for different categories of population; nutrition needs of children and old people; the number of shoes that children need; the number of textbooks, notebooks, and other school supplies that will be needed twenty years hence should not be beyond the ken of current policy formulations, and so on.

All that I have stated here cannot be done without the very simple activities of counting, measuring, and calculating. I have deliberately resisted the temptation to be systematic in asking the questions. By allowing them to stand in the randomness in which they were generated I hope to kindle in the reader the sense of discovery that comes with realising how much we take things for granted and, in so doing, how much we neglect to realise their importance or even the significance of holding them before our gaze and taking control of them or how they impact our lives. All the preceding questions, were one to permit oneself to be exercised by them, will likely lead to a different way of relating to the issues that they raise but to which we never paid attention.

FIVE

Process, Not Outcome:
Why Trusting Your Leader, Godfather,
Ethnic Group, or Chief May Not Best
Secure Your Advantage

Having one's day in court is more important than having one's way there; rules are more important than outcomes and, in all this, only one thing is held to be certain: everyone bears equal risks of losing and winning in all the situations where rules rule.

IN THIS chapter, I would like to dilate on a different aspect of what it is to be modern: what I term the triumph of procedure over outcome. There are different ways in which this tenet is manifested in modern societies. The most popular form is that of the rule of law. Few doubt that the rule of law has not been domesticated in our polities. The only thing we can argue about is whether or not the failure of the rule of law to take root in Africa has to do with African culture or the nature of Africans or with the unfortunate legacy of colonialism in the continent. The option we adopt will affect our prescription for how to install the rule of law in Africa.

We can peremptorily rule out the option concerning the nature of Africans. It is the product of racial supremacist mischief making that some Africans unwittingly embrace when they insist on the quintessential difference of Africans from the rest of the world's peoples. All too often, the adopted option is that African cultures and the rule of law and its entailments are incompatible. Those who subscribe to this view urge us to look inwards and seek indigenous equivalents for the idea of the rule of law and associated institutions, practices, and processes. On the other hand, colonial apologists are quick to point out and celebrate the claim that the rule of law along with its counterpart, liberal democracy, was the centrepiece of the legacy bequeathed to Africa by European colonialism. Africans are too quick to accept this claim and proceed to engage in futile soul searching respecting where the continent went wrong in its failure to safeguard and preserve the gains of this legacy. I differ with this standpoint. Colonialism and its peculiar characteristics in Africa were the principal reason for the failure of the rule of law and liberal democracy to be firmly rooted in Africa. The current situation in the continent represents the bitter harvest of the seeds of destruction sown by colonialism. Although this discussion will not extend to an expatiation of the reasons for my indictment of colonialism on this score, it is important to point it out because our focus in this chapter turns on our collective orientation to the philosophical foundations of both the rule of law and liberal democracy.

The modern era is notorious for its privileging of form over content, process over outcome, procedure over result. Many readers would recall how, when we did high school mathematics, we were always reminded by our instructors of the need for us to submit along with our answers how we worked our way to them; that is, they placed more premium on method than on the answer. On more than a few occasions, we got the answer right but the working wrong. What we are about to expound in this discussion is very much reflective of the mathematical emphasis on method; except that, in this case, we are talking of social relations in the public sphere. We refer to relations, those between citizens and the state, regarding who does and who does not deserve to have access to the reins of power and, once infractions or infringements have been committed either against the state or an individual and by whomever, how such shall be assessed, judged, and, where necessary, sanctioned. The stakes can vary from the gravest regarding who deserves to exercise a polity's power to determine when criminal infractions have been committed and what sanctions should be imposed, to whether or not a creditor is entitled to remedy from a defaulting debtor.

The way that these issues are conducted in the modern setting is by setting up processes and formulating rules. Rules are not peculiar to the moderns: only it is in the modern era that rules became the central focus and following them became almost an end in itself. It is not that outcomes don't matter; it is just that hewing strictly to the procedures laid down is more likely to ensure fairness than a setting in which we are set on obtaining a desired outcome, come what may. Many people, especially in our communities, have problems with this rule-centred manner of proceeding and think that its pursuit often yields injustice. But I propose to explain why this attitude is misplaced and, in the present situation, why we would have a more equitable society if we embraced the process-over-outcome orientation.

In the aftermath of the elections that took place in Nigeria in 2007, the Nigerian press was for quite a while dominated by news of numerous crises arising from the involvement of "godfathers" and the consequences of such involvement in politics. I am not aware of similar reports from other areas of the continent. This is no comfort, though. The absence of news about the role of godfathers in the politics of other African states does not mean that the phenomenon is not present in them. As we shall soon see, the phenomenon has many variants and many of them are easily discernible in many African societies. What is critical is that godfatherism is contradictory to the process-over-outcome schema. The increasing attention focused on this category of players in Nigerian politics provides an excellent foil for the case that we wish to make for the necessity for Africans to embrace another aspect of the modern inheritance: the dominance of process over outcome; the triumph of procedure over results.

What, the reader might wonder, has the phenomenon of "godfatherism" got to do with the supremacy of procedure over outcome in the modern era? An awful lot. It all has to do with who godfathers are and what they do. Ordinarily, godfathers are, at least in my understanding, identified by their role as an accoutrement in Christian baptism. They are adults, other than the parents of the child to be baptised, who are expected to sponsor the godchild at baptism and serve as guarantors who pledge to continue to guide the child in the way of the Lord as he or she grows into pubescence, adolescence, and, ultimately, adulthood. The key idea here is that of sponsorship and, to a limited extent, guardianship. But there is no doubt that the godfather idea that is relevant in the present discussion is that the provenance of which is traceable to the less savoury character of the head of crime families in what is now known worldwide as the Mafia. The godfather in this case also sponsors his family members and guides them in their lives within the family. But in protecting them in the execution of their nefarious activities and shielding them from their just legal deserts, we find a direct link between godfatherism and procedure as represented, in the present case, in law and the administration of justice.

Certainly, I do not wish to suggest that the business of politics in Nigeria is or mimics the criminal venture that the Mafia is usually associated with. I am sure that many who are familiar with Nigerian politics will disagree with me on this score. Let's leave that aside. In any case, Nigeria is not the focus of this discussion. And even if it were true in the Nigerian situation, we cannot say that this is widespread across the continent. But it is definitely part of my aim in this chapter to argue that what the phenomenon represents, especially with regards to the aspect of modernity under consideration here, is to be found everywhere in the continent. However, there are traits shared by both enterprises. They are impatient with rules or act as if rules are incompatible with their respective ventures or that rules are not likely to yield for them the returns that strong arm tactics would likely avail them in rule-less engagements. Rules, to them, are an inconvenience if not, on occasion, an obstacle on the path to the realisation of their ends. Godfathers thrive in environments in which people, in this case, politicians, don't think that they can trust the process that guides, authorises, and selects winners in the enterprise that they participate in to yield outcomes that are favourable to their interests.

Remember we are talking about politics; that range of activities in which the prize is power, its control, and its deployment. Although in its positive dimension the object of power is the promotion of the well-being of the polity and that of its members, jointly and severally, it is easy to see why it would be pursued with verve and why, when it is illicitly secured and perverted to illegitimate ends, the consequences are awful. Unfortunately, in the time since modern politics had been introduced into our communities, we have only known it, for the most part, in its perverted incarnation. This perverted form was the dominant form of politics throughout the colonial period, and things have not been markedly different in the post-independence period. Then, as now, those who tried to hew to the noble aims of politics fell victim to the grabbers. The consequence is that politics has, in our land, evolved into a zero-sum game marked by impatience, lust for, and gargantuan misuses of power.

The legacy of this tragedy shows itself in our populations' widespread lack of trust in the play of rules. If those who play by the rules end up getting short shrift, it is not likely that trust in the efficacy of rule-following will be enhanced. Many people may come to think that the process is permanently flawed and can, therefore, not be trusted. This happens when certain segments of the population, from experience, come to believe that the rules are so rigged that the outcome will never reflect their preferences. Or that the other, often victorious, side does not play by the rules and gets away with it and is even rewarded for so doing. Or it may be the case that the process is okay but is vulnerable to manipulation by its operators.

When either of these reasons occurs, the usual solution is to ensure that one has what in Yorùbá is called a *Babanígbèjó* [literally, an influential sponsor at the hearing who gives one the inside track], that is, a godfather. *Babanígbèjó* is unlike, say, a political party polling agent who is at the counting centre to ensure that his or her party's tallies are correctly represented before the results of an election are announced. Nor is he a lawyer who is there to present and defend the case of his client. He usually is one who has considerable influence in the community concerned and whose word is occasionally law, and even when this is not the case, carries a lot of weight in matters that come before the assembled council of the community. Quite often, his influence may authorise a just outcome, but that is only where he has scruples and decides to ensure that the side whose case has more merit should obtain its just deserts. When this is the case, the *Babanígbèjó*'s quintessential role is subverted, and the need to have him on one's side is attenuated, if not defeated. In fact, a situation in which fairness attends the adjudication of cases, and they are determined by considerations of justice, however those are conceived in the relevant community, and the process for reaching this were set up properly, to have a *Babanígbèjó* would be superfluous, if not subversive. In such a situation, the *Babanígbèjó* becomes ineffective. In other words, there is almost a contradictory relationship between the *Babanígbèjó* phenomenon and due process.

The godfather phenomenon has a million incarnations in the African continent. I have so far referred to its manifestation in the area of politics where the godfathers sponsor candidates in elections, go to any lengths to ensure that their candidates win and, in the aftermath, expect substantial pay-offs in the form of raw cash, preferences in the award of contracts and, in many cases, in selecting members of the executive of the administration that results. We find similar manifestations when someone's influence is required to win court cases, government contracts, beauty contests, admission spots in schools, universities, and even military academies, good grades in educational institutions, and so on.

Although the *Babanígbèjọ́* is always personified, the valence in virtue by which he comes by the influence he has and the power he exercises is not limited to any single factor. He may personify ethnic privilege in a situation in which membership of a given ethnic or national group bestows unearned or unmerited benefits. At other times, he may embody the power that is conferred by his membership of a Lodge, an exclusive social club, a religious denomination, old school network, guild, or trade association. The common denominator is that the *Babanígbèjọ́* does not bother with rules to secure advantages for his clients and himself. Insofar as this is so, we should think of the *Babanígbèjọ́* as an institution that is often personified in the individuals and groups that deploy it to secure their advantage in relevant situations.

However the power comes about, once the factor is interposed in public affairs, it triggers off a domino effect. Everything is affected by it; nothing is left standing. Once functionaries are chosen, not by merit or rules well laid down, it would be too much to expect such functionaries to uphold procedures. Meanwhile, their prospective clients who know or have reason to believe that those who serve them did not obtain their positions by merit cannot be expected to trust in process, either. Hence, the easy resort to rule-subverting manoeuvres like individuals offering inducements to such officials to move their cases ahead of those who came earlier, or tying themselves to mini-godfathers who might be in a position to influence the officials concerned, if they do not go directly to those by whose intercession the officials obtained positions they did not deserve. They tie themselves to the apron strings of other godfathers who are eager to show that they can deliver what other godfathers may not be able to. A whole culture is created in which generations are socialised into believing that they cannot obtain any benefits except by their linkage to godfathers. That this culture of not following rules is now widespread in the continent is evidenced by the fact we now celebrate those who do the right thing for the sheer fact that they do so; that is, doing the wrong thing has become the norm.

What all the preceding instances in their bewildering variety tell us is that in all those situations where the godfather phenomenon and its analogues predominate we have the dire absence of: a culture of process, sometimes called the Rule of Law; widespread faith in the supremacy of procedure; and a fundamental belief that the one who follows the rules of the game will not end up as the loser, irrespective of his or her level of competence in the game. By contrast, in those societies in which rules are substituted for personal influence, where the rule of law replaces the rule of men, where rule-following supplants influence-peddling, where an individual's capacity to "make things happen" is displaced by rule-guided equality of all, people not only do not need to have godfathers or their equivalents, the injection of godfather-types into the process is criminalised and adjudged morally repugnant by the greater majority of the population and attracts severe sanctions, both formal and informal.

In line with the main thrust of the thesis that has informed this book, here again I would like to submit that if the modern age is about anything, it is about the triumph of procedure over outcome. This part of the modern heritage, as indeed other elements that we have identified so far in this discussion, was never part of the package of bequeathals that colonialism handed over to various countries in Africa. If anything, we were handed empty shells of institutions, practices, and processes that lacked the animating and legitimating spirit of their originals in Europe. And like other non-modern societies in other parts of the world, including crucially even some of the countries that colonised Africa—Belgium and Portugal easily come to mind here—many African societies were not characterised by what one might call the "fetishisation" of rules, the placing of process over outcome and the commitment to the putative equality of all. Indeed, under colonial rule, the rulers pointedly insisted that Africans were not capable of recognising, much less celebrating, technicalities, formal rules, and impersonal procedure, which are all integral parts of modernity's claim to supremacy over previous modes of social ordering in history.

And their practice hewed strictly to their contempt for the Africans' ability to follow rules and appreciate the niceties of procedure as embodied in the Rule of Law and the equality of all before the supremacy of rules. This was not limited to the sphere of law. The same practice dominated in the political sphere. Legislators were appointed or selected, not elected. The views of the people, the electorate, counted for nought. Creating responsive and responsible governments was not in the cards. Why a commitment to process and procedure might occasion intractable problems for colonial rulers is not difficult to understand: colonialism is about hierarchy and not the kind of hierarchy that is denominated by merit. In the colonial situation, circumstances of birth, status, and, ultimately, skin colour dictated who ruled and who was ruled. It was rule of men, par excellence.

I am sure that many will be astonished by my insisting that colonialism might have featured what I am calling godfatherism. Yes, it did. Because it did not operate on the rule of law nor did it insist that things be done according to rules, it was not in a position to school those over whom it ruled in the ways of modern rule preference. It chose particular groups as rulers or warriors based on arbitrary considerations. In the colonial situation, white people ruled and dominated regardless of their competence or lack of it. The colonial civil service was filled with people who were recruited on the basis of the say-so of their headmasters, their local politicians, social club members and, when all else failed, their white skin. It was godfatherism run riot!

Ironically, it was not until African leaders who had been schooled in the modern traditions and who themselves owed their ascendancy to merit—which, to be sure, the colonial authorities refused to recognise and severely denigrated—and had chafed under the godfatherism-inflected operations of the colonial system began to run the colonial structure in preparation for self-government that the tradition of placing process over outcome, rules over results, merit over ascription, began to be implanted. But few were those who had imbibed that attitude and, as we know too well, there was little time for the roots to take before the scourge of military and one-party rule began to interfere with and destroy the fortunes of democracy and the rule of law and the regime of rules in general all across the continent. This, ultimately, was the tragedy of colonialism in Africa, one which the continent must undo if it is to move forward with the rest of humanity.

In the countries whence came the operators of the colonial system, they had substituted the rule of law for the rule of men. They did not do so because they loved process more; it was because they loved men less. The rule of men was characterised by caprice, raw power, inequality that was not based on any clear criteria, and so on. There was unpredictability and enormous injustices. Even when justice was served, it could not be relied upon as precedent, and there were no guarantees that future cases that were otherwise similar would yield similar outcomes. Colonialism could not have been a finishing school for the rule of law and its attendant scrupulous adherence to rules and their impartial application in relevant situations. I am arguing that the strict adherence to rules that is the hallmark of the modern age never became part of the political socialisation of Africans under colonial tutelage.

We have in the decades since followed too closely, to our detriment, the playbook of the colonial era as well as antecedents in our various cultures, especially those that weighed more on the side of the rule of men rather than the triumph of procedure. It is important to underscore the fact that the rule of men was not the exclusive heritage of Europeans. Our societies, too, were characterised by the rule of men, merely moderated by appeal to religious and other supernatural sanctions. It was not that there were no rules; it was that we, like peoples the world over, did not live and die by them. We continue to see the play of those rule-of-men antecedents in our societies in the desire of our nationalist thinkers to strengthen various institutions founded on ascription rather than merit: non-elective kingships, succession to which is determined for the most part by heredity, chieftaincies, age-grades, and gerontocracy. Unfortunately, colonialism strengthened those institutions when it could and ought to have weakened them or completely evacuated them of their salience. In exactly the same way that the colonial regimes subverted rules, substituted caprice, and dispensed with technicalities, our societies, especially those that have had the misfortune of prolonged military rule, have never really come to an appreciation of the supremacy of process over outcome.

The fact is that in the modern dispensation, process is absolutised in such a way that substantive justice is sacrificed for procedural justice. Having one's day in court is more important than having one's way there. Rules are more important than outcomes and, in all this, only one thing is held to be certain: everyone bears equal risks of losing and winning in all the situations where rules rule. Where this often does not occur, there exists a case for the process to be re-tuned and distorting influences removed or reduced. The legal system, for example, promises equal access to its institutions and the justice it dispenses; it does not promise that the outcome will favour any particular litigant or group consistently or invariably. There is an element of chance that is built into how the system works even as it is supposed to generate some stability in the expectations of the parties as to outcome. The mistake is that people think that this stability applies to the outcome whereas it only applies to the process. In so far as rules are not applied mechanically, and they are handled by judges and other arbiters who remain human, and therefore limited, contingency will reign supreme. This explains why quite often the outcome seems unjust even when the process has been meticulously observed. People may complain but, for the most part, everyone agrees that the procedural justice that it ensures is far more equitable than the occasional hits that a system of rule by men might happen upon.

It is out of place here to dilate on the theory of human nature that informs the suspicion about the human capacity to always do right. It suffices to reiterate that in the modern era, there is a fundamental skepticism about the capacity of the human mind to know without the possibility of error. As long as this is the case, human knowing will always have to be treated with a dose of skepticism.

Many of our indigenous systems of governance and adjudication appreciated the limits of a system of rule by men. We see it in the fact that very few rulers ever earned the qualifier: "the Great." This is a good reminder to us at the present time that we cannot keep hoping to have the best men at the helm of our affairs. This is a luxury that we can dispense with in a rule regime. We have rules to limit the excesses of men and women. Rule regimes are founded upon a basic skepticism about human nature. Humans are limited by their nature, blinded by ambition, swayed by self-preference, and sometimes the dullness of our cognitive tools leads us astray in judging cases even when we mean to do the best. The formal equality that undergirds the legal and political systems in the modern era is easily distinguishable from substantive equality, and I don't think that those who understand the metaphysics of the self that is deployed in modernity are likely to allow themselves the luxury of mistaking one for the other.

We already saw in chapter 2 that in the modern age all humans are equal. The equality at issue is not of the substantive variety. It is the formal equality of all arising from the sheer fact of their common humanity and it is asserted in spite of the glaring inequalities of birth, physical endowment, class, and so on. When it is claimed that we are all equal before the law or that the law is no respecter of persons, it is this formal equality that is referenced. That is why, as we found out in chapter 2, no individual counts for more than any other individual: there is no natural superiority of any individual or group to another. Each answers to rules that are indifferent to status, nationality, religion, class, period.

To continue with the example of the legal system, consider the principle that everyone is equal before the law; that the law is no respecter of persons. We all know that in its operation, this principle often seems not to be followed to the letter. We know that those with means often receive what look like undeserved breaks in their encounters with the law; for example, easy bail conditions, release in their own recognisance, legal services that enable them to exploit technicalities of which the law contains a plenitude, and so on. Does this fact detract from the cogency of the principle of the equality of all persons before the law? I don't think so.

A principal reason for the institution of the principle can be traced to the need to ensure that those with

means do not have any undue advantage in legal processes that their wealth or standing in the community might
confer on them. If in a system in which a "big man" dominates he could preempt his being dragged before the law
such as it might exist there, but in a system in which the
law is no respecter of persons, he would have to suffer
the indignity of having to report to the law and making a
case for why he should be allowed to go home, even for a
bail-eligible offence. If the rule says that, in recognition
of the dignity of the suspect, which is sometimes tied to
the individual's reputation as an upstanding member of
the community, we should not hold in custody people
who are not flight risks, we may not say that rich people who often easily fall within this category should be
treated differently. Contrary to what many might think,
releasing such people is not a subversion of the rules; it
is indeed a fulfilment of them. Were such a system not in
place, his status would have preempted any proceedings
being commenced against him. On the obverse, even the
poorest of the poor or the weakest of the weak cannot
have a "big man" have them rot in jail or be brutalised in
any way without the instrumentality of the law. And that
instrumentality does not allow unwarranted punishment
for the weak on account of the say-so or influence of the
strong. This is really what shows the double-edgedness of
rules under any condition.

It is easy to accuse me of whitewashing the modern legal and political systems; of painting a rosy picture
of a very flawed system. Again, I offer the defence that I

have deployed repeatedly in this work. I am not sanguine about the many flaws in the operation or even in the conception of the systems in question. But as is the case in all manifestoes, our emphasis here is on the positive, and our aim is not to give comfort to those who do not see anything good in what we offer. I am convinced that those are best situated to point out the flaws of a system who are better educated about its virtues or have had the privilege of enjoying its benefits. I don't believe that Africans have ever had the privilege of enjoying the benefits that modernity and its institutions have to offer. Quite the contrary, the African situation is replete with innumerable instances of reliance on the rule of men rather than that of law and strict adherence to process or procedure.

The executive in the African state is wont to ignore or circumvent procedures, subvert processes, and, generally, interpose the play of influence for the role of rules in decision making, as well as in its dealings with those who work for and in it, the people whose affairs it is charged with administering, and other spheres of the polity in which it is supposed to have no role, much less an influence. The situation is no better with the civil service, an institution that, in the modern state, is supposed to be the embodiment of bureaucratic rationality underpinned by rules and their peremptory powers. To start with, the bureaucracy is supposed to be an institution typified by careers open to talent. That is why civil services around the world are marked by very strong reliance on competitive examinations. Not only is entry into them determined by clear rules, rules constitute a hallmark of a professional civil service. Their loyalty is not to the government of the day; it is to the state that that government is momentarily in charge of; the bureaucracy does not act according to the whims of the temporary occupiers of the helm of the ship of state but according to rules laid down, and this commitment to the rules is without regard to the short-term interests of the party in power. In such situations, citing a relevant or binding rule peremptorily ends the discussion on the issue at stake.

The situation is not much different in our educational institutions, which are charged with the responsibility of socialising their participants at all levels into the embrace of rules, processes, procedures, and the like. What we find instead are instances of male candidates for professorial chairs bartering their wives for advancement, female candidates offering their bodies for favours, students bartering their bodies or monies or goods for grades, and everybody coming to believe that following rules is for fools. When educational institutions, the context for the formation of the character and attitude of those who stand to inherit the captaincy of their societies, become cesspools of rule subversion and hotbeds of godfatherism, it is fair to conclude that such societies are headed for perdition.

Meanwhile ordinary folks are forever offering inducements for powerful officials to rule in their favour, regardless of the merits or lack thereof of their case, hitching their wagons to some "big man's" train in order thereby to ensure that they obtain whatever it is that they want, and the lowliest public official becomes a big-man equivalent just to perform the most ordinary of official functions. I have refrained from commenting on the well-known penchant of law-enforcement agents across the continent for bribes and the repeated subversion of the rules that are supposed to guide their engagement with the public that they are charged with protecting.

One tragic consequence of this proliferation of the rule of men in African countries is the inducement in generations of Africans of a proclivity towards abjection. I make bold to say that Africans are well practised at abjection. Starting with the battery and denigration of our humanity under colonialism to the brutal rule of men in the post-independence period, we have made a culture out of being abject. When we are stopped by policemen, our mien quickly betrays fear that we are caught. We do not demand to know why we are stopped: we shift to the abject mode. We obsequiously greet the officer convinced that if we are prostrate enough, he would have mercy on us. We always act as if we believe that we are guilty of something, even if we don't know what it is. We plead guilty to unknown charges and even before we are told we are being charged with anything.

The absence of rules or the culture of non-adherence to them injects an element of arbitrariness and a culture of impunity on the part of those who wield power: the rules are what they say they are. Those amongst us who insist on their self-respect find out that the transaction costs of pressing their right are quite high, often prohibitive and, at the end of the day, decide that it is not worth it. We often do not think that pressing respect for our dignity is worth life itself. This widespread attitude does not admit of class or other social differences. Godfathers who have fallen out of power are as cowed as the rest of us ordinary people where falling victim to the arrogance and brutality of power in the African context is concerned. To be sure, upper class individuals who are as afflicted as the lowliest of their compatriots are the ones who are likely to deny their abjection. They rationalise their complicity along the following lines: "I don't want that boy to waste my time. What does he want?" They quickly pay the bribe to the man at the illegal check-point and think nothing of the fact that they have just played a part in enabling the culture of *babanígbèjó*ism. The continent is led by mendicant rulers who model abjection to the rest of the world, and their enabling intellectual advisers reinforce their resignation that things could not be different for Africa. Rarely do you find African rulers and their intellectual enablers talk about Africa's future prosperity without some reference or the other to sourcing aid from motley donors including countries which themselves needed aid till recently. The end result is that dependence on aid has stunted Africans' imagination so much that readily available resources for progress are experienced as burdens and a culture of non-responsive and non-responsible government has been installed all across the continent.

What is very clear from the discussion in the last few paragraphs is that the rule of men predominates in our countries. This is evidenced in the fact that, even in the simplest of situations, we are more likely to put our trust in a godfather, a leader, a chief, a big man or woman, our family ties, our friendships, old school ties, ethnic or religious connections—all variations of the *babanígbèjóʼ*ism phenomenon—than in the impersonal operations of rules that are publicly promulgated and expected to be adhered to by everyone, rulers and ruled alike.

In light of the positive picture that I have painted of the sway of rules and processes, it is meet to ask: does process work? No doubt, one may cynically conclude that the fact that African countries continue to survive and, in some cases, prosper under the rule of men is proof that what I have generally put under the category of godfatherism works. Of course, if you are the big man or if the big man is always on your side, it is likely that things will work. Moreover, if you have means and you are able to buy yourself "efficient" disposals of your issues in the state or generally ensure that your preferences and those of your followers are well served, there is no reason for you to think that anything is seriously wrong with things as they are. If, on the other hand, you fall within the ranks of the ordinary masses or the deprived or the middle classes with limited resources to "make things happen" for you and yours, I have no doubt that you will be less enthusiastic about things as they are. Beyond these two broad groups, on balance, the truth of the matter is that those who suffer from the depredations of godfatherism and its equivalents are infinitely more than those prospered by them. It is not even true that godfatherism is as effectual as it is claimed for its sponsors and practitioners.

There are many reasons why godfatherism is dysfunctional or, at least, inefficient. The power of the chief, godfather, leader, or other sponsor, however it is derived, is often a function of the relative lack of power by contending others. To the extent that we can envisage those others obtaining superior power or means—and it is often the case that those others do—it must be clear that the protection offered by our sponsor can only be momentary; until a superior power comes along. We see this often enough in the speed with which yesterday's godfathers are beggared by newly empowered ones in the distribution of spoils and the satiation of followers' wants in the aftermath of changes of administration in African institutions, governmental and others. As soon as there is regime change, we read or hear of reversals of allocations, licences, and other favours. For example, as long as the Sunnis of Iraq had godfather Saddam Hussein in power, they ruled the roost of Iraqi public life. Now new godfathers dominate Iraqi life, and there has been a severe reversal of fortune for Iraqi Sunnis. The godfather motif might be another reason why "tribalism" reigns in Africa. Rules will attenuate, if not remove, the need for "tribal" godfathers and reduce the severest manifestations of the politics of identity without thereby abolishing ethnic/national differences and the cultural pluralism that they entail. Appointments are not exempt, and one cannot sympathise with those who get their comeuppance having themselves been appointed in ways that paid no attention to procedure. The victims, if we can call them that, cannot go to court to seek redress—you cannot go to law when you have been a beneficiary of the breach of laws in the original preferments—a move that is clearly an available remedy in a regime of rules.

Yesterday's vice chancellor with whom you have prostituted your spouse may not be able to secure the advantage you desired should the process not be finalised before he left office and a new one took over. The chief upon whom you depended to ensure that you obtained the contract to supply textbooks may have his power and influence clipped by the substitution in the executive chambers of a different faction of the party. The teacher with whom you have traded your body for grades may fall victim to a scrupulous department chair who ensures that those grades are duly reversed leaving you with nothing but the shame of having sold yourself at all. What is more, there is no guarantee that the one on whom you have chosen or are forced to depend will deliver on his or her promise. He might take advantage of you and leave you high and dry. In a system not founded on process and the enforcement of clearly delineated rules, you are forced to resort to the power of shame or the deployment of superior force, sometimes in the manner of "hired assassins," to redress your grievance. There is evidence that in various parts of the continent the incidence of godfathers sponsoring violence against rivals and their minions has often spiralled out of control, and deals gone bad have often led to the rubbing out by the losers of whoever was advantaged by their loss. How anyone can seriously entertain that such a condition of war is salubrious for the societies caught in that cycle boggles the mind.

Secondly, one of the promises of a rule-based system is the predictability of its processes. There is the guarantee that like cases will be treated alike and prior decisions will circumscribe the limits of later ones. In such a system it is easy for individuals to conform their actions to the parameters set by the relevant rules. In a system in which the say-so of big men and women or their equivalents is law, unless one is in the nearly impossible position of divining the likes and dislikes of the men and women concerned, a quality that does not assure that what they did in the past would be a predictor of what they would do in future situations, it is clear that it would be more difficult, if not impossible, for one to so suit one's behaviour to the demands of such a situation.

Contrast the situations we have just described with what happens in a system characterised by the supremacy of process and rules. Recall what we said earlier about the formal quality of the justice that the rule-based system promises. What is clear is that in that system everyone stands a formal chance of losing as equals.

There is an equalisation of the risk of losing, though not an equalisation of losses. Where the men of means may escape having to plead their cause in a system in which their say-so holds sway, in the process-dominated system, they have to undergo the "indignity" of establishing the merits of their case or proving their innocence. Their risk of losing when their case lacks merit is no less than that of the lowliest member of the society. Even though their chances of winning may be enhanced by their considerable means, they need to expend a lot more of their resources, money and moral, in order to secure such an outcome. One may think that this is not much but when one thinks of what they could get away with in a different dispensation, one might not be so sanguine about their prospects after all. The play of means is neutralised and everyone is invested with the same forbearances in their treatment by the authorities. Everyone is accorded the presumption of innocence in the legal sphere, however rich or poor he or she happens to be.

Thanks to the regime of rules, the police officer is not permitted to take liberties with you even when he or she has a reasonable suspicion that you may be engaged in an illegal activity. The officer may not lay hands on you in the process of arresting you. A single slap would represent an illegitimate abridgment of the separation between the executive, which he represents, and the judiciary, which is a different province from his. His is to collect evidence and build a case. It is the magistrate's responsibility to listen to the case that the police make on behalf of the state and listen to yours and decide who has the force of law and the balance of facts on his side. He may not help himself to your body in the name of a search or to extensions of your person such as your car, your house, your brief case, your handbag, and so on, without his having gone before a judge and made a case that he has reasonable grounds for suspecting that your body may be hiding some contraband. Can you imagine how much less fear ridden our lives would be on the road when a police officer stops us and demands to see what is in our suitcase? In a regime of law, that is unwarranted and illegal search. Given that we are supposed to be presumed innocent until proven guilty in a properly constituted tribunal, it would remain, as it is written in our laws as I write this, illegal for the officer to ask us to account for how the money in our handbag was obtained. Under the doctrine of the presumption of innocence, it is the state that has to lead evidence to show that the money was illegally obtained; it is not ours to prove that we did not steal it.

All our countries have all the laws, regulations, and doctrines that I have just described and illustrated. It is a mark of the dominance of the rule of men that very few Africans can recall when they have been the recipients of the kinds of courtesy that our modern legal system is supposed to extend to us in its dealings with us. What we have instead is the widespread rule of impunity where policemen beat suspects, judges do not open inquiries into suspects' insistence in court that they had been subjected to beatings, even when the ocular proof is right there before the judges' very eyes, and there is no possibility that there might be a future date when those who perpetrated violence against citizens in the name of the state would be called to account for their crimes and misdemeanours.

In case anyone thinks that rule following is only required for the state-citizen relationship, I would like to point out that that is not the case. Rules are also required to structure interpersonal relationships. Once you are clear that the law will enforce a duly enacted contract, you would not need any strong-arm tactics when there is non-performance by the other party to the contract. The landlord-tenant relationship does not have to degenerate into the landlord literally hiring a mason to take the roof off to get rid of an obdurate tenant, and the tenant does not have to hire thugs to teach an obnoxious landlord a lesson. The rules for tendering for contracts will be clearly announced, and the conduct of the opening of tenders and awarding the contract can be seen to be above board.

Finally, a critical difference between a godfather-inflected system and a process-dominated one is that in the latter, the transaction costs of subverting process are quite high. They include, but are not limited to, imprisonment, monetary fines, forfeitures, loss of entitlements, and good old social opprobrium. And rules are like elephants: they do not forget. Except where there are clear provisions for time limitations, no wrongdoer can rest easy, as long as he or she is alive, that the rules will not catch up with him or her. Wouldn't it be nice for Africans who have been victims of the misrule of men in their polities to know that they could look forward to some day in the future when good old nemesis will catch up with their tormentors, torturers, appropriators of their common inheritance and the latter will receive their just deserts? For reasons adumbrated in this section, I conclude that process does work, and I would like to contend that an Africa dominated by the strict adherence to procedure, an absolutisation of the play of rules and principles, and an abandonment of the rule of men and women—godfatherism/*Babanígbèjó*ism, as we have termed it—will be a much better continent whose peoples will be much better served by the creation of humane conditions of life and thought for all.

At the beginning of this discussion, we pointed out that the choice of the rule of law and principle over the rule of men and women was not compelled by a love of law or rules but by a basic suspicion about human nature. The grounds of this suspicion have been supplied in chapter 2. In fact, part of what is wrong with trusting our fortunes to the generosity and kindness of sponsors, leaders, godfathers, or chiefs is that, as was said above, we cannot be sure that their aid would not exact too high a price from us or that it would not end up rendering us inferior to those upon whose largesse we depend. The rule of men breeds abjection which, in turn, is an affront to human dignity, and a subversion of the equality of all. It is usually said that beggars are not choosers. How true! What is more, given the many ways in which the reliance on our fellows may be misplaced, it stands to reason that one who thinks deeply about the issues will be a bit queasy about reposing confidence in his or her fellows.

Of greater significance is the historical fact that at the dawn of modernity, the principal motivation for the institutionalisation of the supremacy of procedure and process could be traced to a fundamental lack of confidence in the basic goodness of human nature. The founders of modern philosophy theorised that humans are forever hostage to self-preference and that what was required was to create a system of governance that would neutralise, given that it could not eliminate, the sway of self-preference in the design and operation of the institutions of the modern polity. Africans are not different from this flawed humanity. The radical difference of Africans from the rest of humanity is the product of the demented imagination of racists and their unwitting African water-carriers at the present time. All the prattle about African communalism does not change one whit of this truism. The dominance of procedure and the rule of law were designed to curb the tendency towards self-preference and ensure, in light of modernity's founders' proclamation of the formal equality of all, that no one person or group of persons, however rich or well circumstanced, could coerce the will of another without the consent of that other. When we look at the societies where this principle has become well entrenched, we discover that they are, for the most part, the societies that many desire to live in around the world. While I do not attribute every success of those societies to their embrace and celebration of procedure, I surely would contend that it is a very important part of that story. This is where the lesson for Africa is to be found.

Six

Against the Philosophy of Limits: Installing a Culture of Hope

A culture of hope is tied to a horizon of time, an ontology of time in which the future is dominant, the past and the present are mere way stations on the path to a future that always promises more and better for both the self and the many groups and contexts in which this self unfolds and operates to realise its goals.

IN THIS chapter, I propose to explore the last tenet of modernity that is of moment in this discussion: the open future. We started out with the idea of individualism. We showed that the individual is the core piece of the modern age. Almost everything is geared towards ensuring the flourishing of the individual. It is not that the group does not matter; it is that the relationship between the individual and the group does not privilege the group and is expected to be contingent, a product of negotiation. This is the only way that the idea of governance by consent has meaning and relevance. Beyond that, we saw that the individual was not tethered to the circumstances of her birth, that is, to the social station of the family into which she was born. On the contrary, whatever situation she was born into, the promise of the modern age is that this individual is called upon or made to realise and routinely reminded that her life is hers to make, her biography is not a closed book the chapters of which could pretty much be read out of her family background. Rather her life is always ahead of her; it is for her to make of it what she will. In other words, she is not captive to her past and, as long as she is willing to strive, the future is hers to shape, design, and realise. She could be whatever she wants, limited only by her talents and how hard she is willing to work for her future. This is what the idea of the open future stands for.

The open future brings us to a dimension of modernity that has been lurking in this discussion so far: a definite orientation to time. The open future is a horizon of time. It is a horizon dominated by the notion that the best is yet to come and that each new day presents new possibilities for world making; both the world of the individual and that of the group. It is the expectation that things can always be better, and it is the responsibility of individuals, proud possessors of reason, capable of using reason to control and manipulate nature, to set to work and remake their world. This is the idea of progress and the unrelenting faith in its possibility that dominates modernity.

I would like to argue that this idea of progress has not been a part of the African imaginary; at least, not since formal colonialism was clamped on the continent in the aftermath of the Berlin West African Conference of 1884–85. We have solid historical evidence that in different parts of the continent, especially in West Africa at the beginning of the nineteenth century, under missionary sponsorship, some Africans had been inducted into modernity and had themselves embraced its basic tenets. As a consequence, they had initiated a transition to modernity that would later be aborted by the imposition of colonialism. No doubt, they, too, had bought into the metaphysical package that included all the elements that have so far featured in this manifesto crowned, ultimately, by their fervent embrace of the idea of progress and their enthusiasm for remaking their societies in the modern image. Their march to progress was stymied and their ambitions were frustrated by the reactionary colonial administrators who insisted that Africans belonged to the infancy of the human race and, therefore, could be trusted neither to appreciate what modernity has to offer by way of new ways of being human nor to run their own affairs. The failure the contours of which we have been delineating in this manifesto must be traced to this abortion, and there is no doubt that the current dismal state of the continent is in part the bitter harvest of the sorrow seeds sown by the colonial administrators.

Unfortunately, we ourselves have played a principal role in this tragedy by our failure to interrogate the legacy of colonialism, falsely equating it with modernity, and shunning the latter in the mistaken belief that what is required for us to move forward is to negate whatever we think is associated with or may have been tainted by the colonial experience. This is a mistaken identification, and it is one that has cost and continues to cost Africa dearly. We run institutions bequeathed to us by colonialism and we have not thought fit to dispense with them in the years since independence. Yet we foolishly refrain from engaging with the modernity-inflected philosophical templates from which were forged the institutions, practices, and processes that have since dominated our lands and lives. It has been the entire purpose of this manifesto to press home the necessity of our embracing the modern way of life so that we can redeem for Africans the benefits of modernity. An integral part of this call is the embrace of the idea of progress under which the open future challenges us to rise up against the philosophy of limits, which has since colonial times dominated our lives, and, instead, install a culture of hope.

A culture of hope is tied to a horizon of time, an ontology of time in which the future is dominant, the past and the present are mere way stations on the path to a future that always promises more and better for both the self and the many groups and contexts in which this self unfolds and operates to realise its goals. The remaking that the idea of progress involves requires its ultimate author to be a self-directed, self-making individual who herself never is but is always becoming. Identity is not given by history nor set once and for all at birth or by affiliation to an ethnic or national group, religious faith or denomination, birthplace, and so on. The individual chooses. Citizenship is portable. New autobiographies and identities are always possible.

The modern spirit is marked by restlessness: its denizens are always on the move. A new formation, a new personality, a new identity is always on offer and just around the corner. Repose is equated with death and stagnation. Optimism is the only currency; there is little or no room for despair. Whatever does not work shall soon pass away. Newness is forever new. The ontology of time at issue here can be captured in the Yorùbá proverb: *Òní la rí, kò sẹ́dà tó mọ̀la* [tr.: We are witnesses to the present; no one knows what tomorrow has in store.] There are other variations of this proverb including one that ends thus: Only God knows the future. I have elected to appropriate this proverb in its more progressive construal. It is sometimes used in a fatalistic sense whereby we are counselled to resign to what fate will make tomorrow bring for us; wait on the Lord and trust he will do right by us. In this alternate meaning, agency is repudiated; the individual is dethroned from the subject position. In its more progressive meaning, yesterday's dead and gone; today is already upon us; tomorrow is ours to make. There is no predestination, no locked up outcomes. Fate is a myth. Ours is always to look for the next breakthrough: the future is ours to make.

Have we in Africa apprehended this ontology of time? Does it inform our personal, public, and institutional lives? Do we exhibit some of the traits that we find in other societies which have embraced the modern idea? For example, modern society does not fix things because they are broken but because they are old and static. The aim is always to renew things, give them new lives or new identities. Make them, at a minimum, look different. Sometimes all that is changed is the façade but the idea of leaving the structure as it is is just not good enough. This is not an integral part of our consciousness in Africa.

What is more, we do not approach the future with a can-do sense of optimism. We are more likely to announce our acquiescence in whatever fate, nature, God, our godfathers, and so on bring our way where the future is concerned. This attitude of resignation is the dominant mindset in Africa. We have our presidents thanking God for their elections. They may be right, since many of those elections are not won via established rules and processes that could be objectively ascertained. It may be that the reason for their electoral victory is opaque to the winners, too, and therefore falls into the realm of the inexplicable, a miracle or, at least, a wondrous product of the mysterious ways of the Lord or some other inscrutable agent. This attitude breeds on the part of many Africans, regardless of their social location, a culture of resignation, of reconciling with things as they are, as foreordained and, therefore, impervious to their tinkering. Faith in the efficacy of human tinkering comes with the modern idea and is crucial to the constitution of the modern identity. The modern consciousness acknowledges that it cannot do anything about the past; but the future is open to tinkering. Success awaits the explorer. I believe that it is way past time that Africans embraced this idea with both hands and ran with it.

It was several years ago. I was teaching at the then University of Ife, now Obafemi Awolowo University. As I was wont to do, I would go into class and exhort my students to always strive to better themselves, to never fail to develop their talents, however modest they were, and that the only limit they had to contend with both in my class and, by extension, in life, was that of their own imagination. I would say that I did not have a set number of A's to hand out in the courses that I taught: if the whole class did "A" work, I wouldn't refrain from so accrediting their work; if, on the other hand, they did "F" work, I wouldn't flinch from flunking the entire class. The idea that I had then and still do now is that no student who sits in my classes and is willing to work tirelessly for it is precluded from obtaining the top grade obtainable.

Needless to say, I expected that not all of my students would buy into my idea, although I wished that enough of them would believe it and take it seriously enough to have it positively impact their lives. One day, one of them, let's call him Móládé, walked into my office after a class session in which I had made my usual pitch to him and his cohort. He said to me: "Malam, do you really believe what you were telling us in class just now?" I replied, "of course, I do, wholeheartedly." He volunteered that he did not and could not share my belief. "Why not?" I asked. He proceeded to offer me his alternative account of why some must have A's and others D's. "We are all born," he said, "with different *Orí* [literally: heads], a product of nature. Some have 'A' *Orí*, others 'B' *Orí*, and yet others 'D' ones, and so forth." I promptly interjected, in light of what up to that point I had noticed was the outcome of his performances on the assignments that he had done in the class: "And you obviously think that yours is a 'D' *Orí*." He did not disagree. "Mọláadé," I said, "I can see from your previous assignments that you are a poor speller. That is not a hindrance to superior performance. Some of the best thinkers and writers in history have been poor spellers. You are also not careful in your writing. What you need to do is give yourself sufficient lead off time when you need to write essays and have a classmate, friend, or associate who is better at spelling go over the piece carefully for you. For the rest come in and consult with me as often as you need to organise your ideas and articulate them clearly. Finally, you have to believe that you can do better and resolve, through hard work, to do so."

No, I do not wish to claim a miracle. Nevertheless, I am happy to report that his fortunes changed dramatically, not just in my class, but also in the others that he was taking, such that at our examiners' board meeting at the end of the succeeding semester, he was singled out for attention. Colleagues wanted to know that he had come by his new academic muscles not by steroids but by honest, hard work in the intellectual gymnasium. I spoke for him and remarked how proud I was that his improvement had been across the board and, therefore, represented a comprehensive change in his life.

Móládé's story is typical of an orientation to life and work that dominates thinking and acting across wide swaths of the African mindscape. While it is easy to trace the genealogy of the orientation to religion, I think that such an account would be mistaken. It is a metaphysical orientation that accounts for the distribution of fortunes and misfortunes, especially in the areas of individual strivings, successes, and failures, in terms of natural, not necessarily occult or religious, forces that act in spite of human preferences or desires. This should not surprise us in a culture in which the individual is a problematic presence. The "A" *orí* owner is inexplicably blessed in exactly the same way that the "D" *orí* owner is equivalently cursed by their respective inheritances. Yes, one may strive but such is the overwhelming influence of this natural distribution that no striving will appreciably alter the fortunes of the "D" *orí* owner. Striving can only marginally affect one's fortunes, so goes the thinking of one caught in the grip of this ontological commitment. This commitment is widely distributed in our societies, and it is embraced not just by the Móládés of this world but by our leaders in all areas of life—politics, industry, academia—even when the evidence of their biographies undercuts the play of nature in their own lives.

Serious consequences arise from this orientation. People and lands that are dominated by it are unlikely to be guided by optimism about their condition and may be inclined to resign themselves to the machinations of fate. What is more, for people in the grip of this attitude, the future becomes a closed book, its unfolding "a chronicle foretold," and the lives of individuals consigned to infinite replications of past divisions of fortunes and misfortunes and the naturalisation of class and status boundaries. This may explain why even those who have excelled by dint of hard work, especially when they have been possessed of what at best are modest talents, do not claim credit for themselves but are forever quick to ascribe their good fortunes to God's inscrutable munificence. Here there is no celebration of talent, of individual initiative, of the quirky genius of the trailblazer; no, it is all God's work or that of inscrutable fate. On the contrary, there is a steady contempt for any such self-recognition, and the strictures on individualism mean that there is a reluctance to celebrate individual genius. We, for the most part, adopt a levelling attitude.

Similarly, when failure is the outcome of their striving, there is no claim of responsibility; no *mea culpas* are forthcoming, no serious effort to trace the cause of failure to possible human errors, individual screw-ups, the play of mediocrity, shoddy organisation, not having matched the right individuals with the right positions, not having exercised necessary quality control over the procurement of materials, and so on. It is easy to see the impact of this mindset in our everyday life. We do not conduct autopsies to establish the cause of death in most cases. This is particularly problematic when such deaths are sudden or when their frequent occurrence ought to clue us into what could be a trend traceable to genetic defects running in families, or abnormalities in newborns and infants that available knowledge already enables us to correct through relevant interventions.

We don't endeavour to find out the causes of events. We already know: God, nature, or the machinations of the wicked. It does not matter how the deaths come about or in what magnitude. Plane crash, automobile accident, or a building collapse, it really does not matter. We buy aeroplanes and operate airlines but we never invest in the domestication of the knowledge base that will enable us to isolate the cause of plane crashes. We buy automobiles but we never invest in the domestication of the knowledge base that will enable us to reduce the incidence of accidents, deaths, and dismemberments on our roads through learning the behaviours of those who drive, the variations brought about by age—young versus old drivers—sex, marital status, level of education, state of health, maintenance culture, beliefs about automobiles, and the relationship between those beliefs and the drivers who go on the road and operate the motor vehicles.

Of course, I am aware that in more tragic occurrences inquiry panels are often set up. But, I suspect, part of why the results of many of those panels never see the light of day, much less have their recommendations implemented to prevent future tragedies, may issue from the self-same attitude that will not countenance causal accounts based on empirical explanations of the previous tragedy informed by exhaustive investigation and superior knowledge. Here we come to the crossroads where the ideas of individualism, of knowledge, and of the importance of counting converge.

To conduct serious investigations requires the kinds of knowledge base that most of our societies never or rarely invest in and, as a result, lack. We also require a different attitude towards the idea of the individual; one that takes selfhood and its attributes, especially that of personal responsibility, very seriously. By so doing we would be in a position to inquire into whether there is individual culpability in the causation of any single incident occasioning death. The degree of culpability, too, will need to be established along the spectrum from wanton disregard or utter recklessness, to negligence, omission, or inadvertence. Some outcomes will require severe or mild sanctions while others will necessitate the altering of working conditions, the provision of better and more up-to-date equipment, and yet others might force us to upgrade training for the relevant personnel.

For us to do any of the preceding things, we would need to establish at some level whether the incidents involved are isolated or their occurrence points towards a trend. If the latter, we are forcibly reminded, once again, of the importance of counting. How many deaths have occurred on a particular stretch of road over a given period of time? If, for example, we find that there is a higher incidence of serious accidents involving automobiles and pedestrians at a particular traffic intersection, we will need to flag that intersection. We may then commission a study to establish whether our hypothesis regarding the emergence of a trend is plausible and what should be done about it: put traffic calming devices on the road, install a new traffic light, paint a new pedestrian crossing there, reduce the speed at which automobiles move through the area, or, in the most drastic cases, put a pedestrian bridge or reroute the road entirely.

Our mindscape is dominated by the philosophy of limits; we apprehend the world in terms of what we cannot do. By contrast, the modern era is the era of excessive optimism, and this not just about the human condition but about humanising the world more and more to make human life meaningful, enjoyable and thoroughly rewarding. This optimism is well-founded. It is built on a history of repeated success in figuring out the "whats," "whys," and "hows" of events and processes. We have been able to recreate, manipulate, block, and vary the causes if we didn't like the previous outcomes. That is why science and the querulous mindset it fosters are central to the modern age.

Optimism breeds a culture of hope that assures individuals that their strivings will not be thwarted by inscrutable forces and that how well or ill they do in their lives is pretty much a function of their striving, however modest their talents may be, however bad a hand nature's lottery has dealt them. In fact, it is not an exaggeration to say that the modern agenda is not merely to reduce the play of nature, chance, fate, or what have you, in human life; it is principally to place humans at nature's control. This attitude is best captured by Albert Einstein's quip that he was desirous to know "the mind of God." We, on the other hand, want only to do the bidding of God's mind. Why would Einstein want to know God's mind? In order that humans might replicate the processes and on occasion succeed in blocking those that promise death and destruction on a mass scale, or just to unravel how things work and why they work the way they do. Given the immensity, if not infinity, of God's mind, it follows that the search for knowledge informed by the modern attitude will be almost endless. *Apropos* what we said in chapter 3 regarding the need to know for its own sake, that analogy with God's mind means that we must risk finding out even when we are not clear what problems the product of our search will help us to solve. This reinforces our strictures on limiting our search for knowledge to solving existing problems.

Thanks to this orientation, the future is never closed nor can it be presaged in the circumstances of the past. The future is always open: it never is; it is always becoming. We don't sit idly by and accept the hand that nature has dealt us. On the contrary, we are called upon to take that hand and make it yield more for us than merely accepting it could do. We do not let tomorrow

take care of itself. We configure or shape it to our preference. Even when our natural endowments turn out to
be modest, we set about making them achieve more than
they would have had we not intensified our exploitation
of them. We think up inventions to turn deserts green.
We study the soil and weather patterns, the genetic constitution of plants to see which ones are hardy enough
to thrive in harsh soil conditions and then see how we
obtain maximum yield from the littlest layout of materials. So, even if we assume with Móládé that his is a "D"
orí, it does not follow that it could not do "C" work, with
appropriate striving and help from teachers, or "F" work,
if it does not even represent its dismal talent in the most
positive light.

The attitude described thus far is widely distributed across the continent and is one of the most effective
markers of the failure of modernity to be rooted in the
African consciousness. Take the current state of affairs in
the continent regarding the issue of Africa's poverty. In
the last thirty years or so, to take an arbitrary time frame,
I have not heard a single African ruler take issue with
what they all now accept is Africa's almost natural poverty. Yet, when we examine the continent's natural, yes,
natural endowments, we find that few other continents
are as fortunately circumstanced as Africa is and always
has been. It may be that the inattention to counting is
holding us back here, too. It takes only a cursory look at
the figures that are often cited for the continent's natural

resources to realise that if there is one continent that has all it requires from nature to flourish, it is Africa.

The continent is home to a handful of the world's major rivers—Nile, Niger, and Congo. The rain forests are being depleted at an alarming rate and, no thanks to our inability to conduct a proper census of the flora and fauna that inhabit those forests, we are not alarmed, as we should be, by their decimation and the attendant elimination of biodiversity that comes with deforestation. Apart from the inherent benefits of preserving the rain forests, we are losing out on the preservation of resources that are requisite to keep our earth in balance and preserve it for future generations. We do not track the possibilities of clean power generation using Africa's bodies of water, falls, and geothermal resources. We are losing our freshwater reserves by the day, and while we make efforts at combatting desertification, the beggaring of our universities and research institutions means that we do not possess the material bases for knowledge production, processing, retrieval, and consumption about desertification and other natural disasters that stand in the way of redeeming the promise of better lives for our people.

Should any proof be needed that we experience the world in terms of limits and our inheritance as a burden, all we need to do is look at current discussion in which Africa's resources are routinely described as Africa's unrelenting curse; where the discovery of oil in commercial quantities in Ghana became a cause for lamentation that the country's people are about to be visited by the "curse of the black gold" and the export of oil in Chad has witnessed the intensification of civil strife in the region; where Congo's resources have always been at the bottom of the unspeakable suffering that humanity has endured there from the days when the Belgian's king's minions hacked off Congolese limbs for not fulfilling their quota of rubber harvests to the present time when bandits protecting their control of diamond and copper mines rape women by the thousands to show who is boss.

Here is the problem: as long as those who have charge of Africa's fortunes, especially those who govern the continent, in light of the centrality of government in the overall lives of Africans and their countries, believe that nature has been unkind to them and their land or that Africa and Africans have been assigned a "D" *orí*— countries, too, in the metaphysical tradition under reference in this discussion, have their *orí* assignations—it stands to reason that they are less likely to strive to shake off this tag of being the self- and historically-appointed beggars to the rest of the world. Even when they permit themselves to strive, their resident doubt regarding what they accept as their lot in life is likely to undermine the confidence with which they otherwise would have sallied forth in the war to conquer hunger, ill-health, and ignorance all over the continent. No thanks to this attitude, Africans are disinclined to make their countries attractive destinations for other human beings from other parts of the world who desire to live out their conceptions of the good life in Africa because the continent offers them the best or, at least, sufficient promising means of doing so.

It is not just African rulers who model the mindset that Africa's backwardness is almost God-ordained. We find a similar attitude abroad among Africa's intellectuals. To start with, we intellectuals are overly enthusiastic enablers of our mendicancy-addled rulers. We exhibit the same proclivity towards the philosophy of limits when we talk interminably about how Africa's problems are so complex that they all but defy solutions, including those that have worked for similar problems in other parts of the world. The only problem is that we also, for the most part, insist that Africa is so radically different from other parts of the world that it makes it irrelevant to talk about adapting other peoples' solutions: *prima facie,* our problems and their problems are not the same. We always look, not at what enables us, but what disables us, and we agree with our rulers—our patrons—that Africa's problems can only or ultimately be solved by divine intervention.

This is why in recent times, African rulers have sponsored national days of prayer, exhorted their peoples to pray more and harder, and many of them have resident spiritual advisors and professional prayer warriors working for them, sometimes at public expense. Some among them have found their way to see particular pastors either in thanksgiving or for intercession with God on their behalf. It is so bad that we don't even think that our soccer teams can win games in international competitions unless God so wills it. And, of course, there is a surfeit of spiritualists with direct lines to God who can assure victories, regardless of the skill levels of our teams and how shoddy their preparations may be! And we wonder why the rest of the world don't respect us.

One only needs to read the writings by African intellectuals and the counsel that we offer to our societies and governments when it comes to solving Africa's gargantuan problems and redeeming the promise of life more abundant for the continent's peoples. Such counsel is full of fulminations about the lingering impact of colonialism and, even earlier, the Atlantic Slave Trade and Slavery. We are not invested in Africa. We do not write for an African audience. The preponderant percentage of our intellectual output is designed for our foreign audience and external sponsors. We do not talk to or with one another in the continent. Our discourses are about Africa but do not unfold in or near Africa. We are enmeshed in a world grid dominated by the needs of external forces. We ought to know that outside prestige and foreign-derived bylines do not translate into relevance for our homeland. What we do is only of benefit to Africa in an oblique manner.

It is thus no surprise that we are all too eager to play the game of our erstwhile colonisers and their successor intellectuals in Euro-America, in which Africa is the sum of its pathologies and we, too, unwittingly become, like them, merchants of misery, forever lamenting Africa's fate and urging the most timid solutions to those problems. Unfortunately, this orientation percolates to the upcoming generations that are schooled in Africa's educational institutions, and they, too, come up the pike with a dismal view of Africa's prospects. We kill their imagination. Their imagination is impoverished, and their purview never extends beyond that of what the continent must do to deserve more aid from its donors and marginally to improve the living conditions of Africans. As for themselves, they inherit the mendicant mentality that suits them for doing what they must in order to attract funding from metropolitan centres. I don't know why it has not dawned on Africans that going elsewhere with no solid foundation at home leaves one vulnerable to being co-opted by the host formation or that if the welter of laurels that we have garnered from foreign hosts in the half a century in which we have sought favours from our colonial rulers has not moved us appreciably closer to being able to stand on our own two feet; it is well past the time for us to look inwards and live or die by our own lights. If we die—subjectivity does not mean that your choices will enable you to live—we would at least die our own death and die with our dignity intact. Being modern means forswearing abjection; assuming autonomy means sometimes going to bed hungry because your dignity will not let you eat humiliation for dinner!

Let me recall another anecdote that illustrates the point at issue here quite clearly. The incident took place in Nairobi in 2000. I had just finished making a presentation on some African intellectuals who, in the nineteenth century, had tried their hands at making African societies over in the modern image by authoring a constitution based on liberal democratic principles and formally adopting the charter for the governance of their community. As should be obvious to the reader by now, I was quite laudatory in my evaluation of their efforts and quite critical of how current generations of African intellectuals, faced with a similar challenge to move Africa along the modern path, this time in the twilight of the twentieth century and the dawn of the twenty-first, had dropped and continue to drop the ball too many times. During question time, a young lecturer took issue with my argument. He asked, "Why do you think that we in Africa have to become like the West to progress?" I replied that I would like to ask him another question before I answered his. He graciously allowed me to proceed. "Do you have any problem with Africa being like the West?" I queried. "Yes," he replied. I curtly rejoined, "Well, I don't." The exchange ended there but the issue did not. He had equated my call for Africa to embrace liberal democracy founded on the principle of governance by consent with a call to be like the West.

Afterward four undergraduate students who had witnessed the exchange challenged me to explain what I meant by my rather impatient answer to my questioner. It turned out that, if my memory serves me correctly, at least one of them was an economics major. As at the time the conference held, Denmark, one of Kenya's major and most generous aid donors had just suspended the transfer of $2 million in aid to Kenya on account of what the Danes decided was the Kenyan government's failure to fight the scourge of corruption, in particular, some allegations of misappropriation of previous aid given to Kenya by the Danish government. The direction of my exchange with the students, over the course of more than one hour, went along the following lines. I asked them which country is richer when it comes to natural resources: Denmark or Kenya. They all agreed that on paper Kenya is richer than Denmark. Then, I asked them why they thought that it was okay for Kenya to be approaching Denmark with a begging bowl. Had they considered that there was nothing in the scheme of things that said that Kenya might actually not be in a position to extend aid to Denmark? No, I didn't think that this was going to happen; the rest of Europe would ensure that things never came to such a pass! It would be considered an affront to the supremacist pride of Europe to allow Europeans to be beholden to Africans for their well-being. Europeans take care of their own but seldom talk about it; Africans do not take care of their own as much as they should but talk interminably about doing so.

What I was doing was to challenge the young minds who had given me the privilege of explaining my stand to them to dream big, impossible dreams. One fundamental reason that Africans are content to be beggars is that we do not permit ourselves to dream impossible dreams, and those among us who do are quickly shut down as "unrealistic" people. In other words, leaders—

political and intellectual alike—exhort their people to be "realistic," a euphemism for "accept your lot and don't think that there is much that you can do to change what has been foreordained." It is the mindset that I illustrated with the anecdote about Móládé earlier in this chapter.

I challenged the young minds to take seriously the privilege of their being educated to become part of that vanguard in Africa that would seek to make African spots must-see places in the world where humanity can come and be prospered just as long as people are willing to work for it. Needless to say, I don't think that safari trips count; nor do aid trips by celebrities or "saviour" young Euro-Americans and their anthropologistic teachers or World Mission types. They should aspire to be the twenty-first century equivalents of nineteenth century African thinkers who dreamed of Africa moving in tandem with the rest of the world on the road to progress. They should dream impossible dreams and challenge themselves to think of ways to realise them. I think that I was able to place my challenge before the students and I was inspired by their openness to a dialogue that few of my colleagues would want to engage in.

The continent has not been without dreamers of the impossible. At the top of that list one must place Kwame Nkrumah and, closely following, Obafemi Awolowo, of Ghana and Nigeria, respectively. It was Nkrumah who wrote profusely about the need to unite Africa under one flag as a precondition for welding its motley peoples and cultures as well as its huge natural resources into an unbeatable world force. Lesser minds among his peers who were forever happy to play self-appointed beggars to the rest of the world dismissed him as a megalomaniac who was only interested in self-aggrandisement. It was completely lost on them that however much Nkrumah might have deluded himself into thinking that he could direct in all details the outcome of the process he was initiating, the fact remained that Africa's many unviable resources and people-poor but flag-hugging states would forever be beholden to their erstwhile colonial overlords for their budget if they, as in the case of Kenya, in spite of their relative wealth of natural endowment, were not part of a larger African community and, by extension, market. He talked about the paradox of the richest continent in natural resources being home to the poorest inhabitants. The challenge faced by Nkrumah and others who thought like him was how to bridge the gulf between the wealth of the continent and the poverty and abjection of its inhabitants.

This is the challenge that is no longer a dominant part of the discourse in the continent, especially among its intellectuals and political leaders. What would happen if, instead of our wallowing in Africa's misery and feeling sorry for ourselves or having the rest of the world feeling sorry for us, we decide instead to face the challenge squarely and dream of moving Africa forward along a path that would make it a desirable stop for whoever in the world is looking for a better life? In other words, what if instead of Kenya forever thinking of adjusting its politics and policies to fit the demands of deserving hand-outs from a generous Denmark, her leaders thought of creating the conditions to take advantage of the country's resources to benefit its peoples? To start with, it would stop thinking of merely feeding itself and rather of being a net exporter of food. It would stop thinking in terms of the fortunes of its "staple food."

I wonder what the staple food of the Danes is. They probably had one in the past but such is the complexity of their culture now that variety marks their diet. Yes, they still have some special dishes that define their national cuisine but I doubt that this will be at the bottom of the culinary order. The more advanced a civilisation is, the greater the likelihood that its national dish would be eaten once in a while and at very great expense. "Staple" means nature or close to it; backward, a lack of variation, simple, just-keep-life-going diet! It bears no mark of quality; it aspires to no luxury or elevation of taste. Because our horizon remains locked at the level of the simple we are still enmeshed in the morass of staple foods that, I bet, are not conducive to a good diet for the most part. Abandoning this investment in the minimum would entail a departure from the stupid romanticisation of small landholding farming to exponentially increasing the yield per acre of fewer farmers and freeing up the energies of many others for work in other sectors of an expanding economy.

Needless to say, all the other aspects that we speak of in this manifesto will kick in. Think of it, if we would address our minds to it and decide to recover our pride in the process, it can be argued that the land and water resources of Nigeria, Democratic Republic of Congo, Ethiopia, and Sudan suffice, between them, to grow enough food to feed Africa and make the countries net exporters of food. Why don't we ever think of producing enough power from the continent's hydroelectric resources to enable us sell power to points in Europe and Asia? Unfortunately, even South Africa, a country that should embody optimism and hope more than any other, is beginning to fall victim to the perennial alibi for impotence in its history. All of a sudden I read of Ireland building low-cost housing for South Africa's poor! Need I say more? And when I saw the shacks that the new administration in South Africa built for its black folks in the name of housing relief in Grahamstown, I could only conclude that it was not only a travesty, indeed, it was a crime. I see similar conditions in other African countries that I have visited. Why don't African leaders think of creating conditions for more of their own peoples to be homeowners? Because, they must think, Africans' *orí* are not of the homeowner variety! Nor is the situation helped by the faux communalism that defines much of the African mindscape.

Let us bring this section of the discussion to a close. I am at the Frankfurt International Airport. I have just gone past the last ritual checking of passports and boarding passes preparatory to boarding the plane that would take me to Washington, D.C., United States of

America. Of course, there is nothing unusual about what I just said. But, unlike all previous occasions, I was struck by the motley crowd of people who work at most airports in the so-called Western countries. Needless to say, given what we know of the labour situations in those countries as well as the division of labour warranted by intensifying pressures brought about by globalisation, one does not remark the overwhelming presence of immigrants from the global south in the janitorial corps of the airports. Yet one must remark the sheer heterogeneity of even the white-collar operatives and the occasional presence of non-Caucasians among the bureaucrats—police, customs, immigration—who staff the ports.

The gentleman who checked my boarding pass and passport just before I boarded triggered these reflections. He must be North African or Asian. I strongly suspect that he was Somali or Eritrean. He works at a German location, which means that his languages of work are German and English, the latter being the language in which he addressed me. Of course, he assumed, wrongly, that I know no German. This also means that he most likely has an original language and some proficiency, if not fluency, in one or another language of the land of his birth. Having been born and reared in a polyglot environment where it was not uncommon for ordinary folk to speak as many languages and dialects as do the people they interact with in their daily lives, I could easily understand the fellow's ease at shifting registers.

What has prompted these reflections is that the countries of the so-called West are typed in the African imagination, mostly among scholars, as places where it is a curse to be black or African, Asian, or what have you; where endemic racism means that the only jobs easily available to them are in the janitorial sector; and where Africans are forever restricted to "ghetto" living. But I am not interested in the correctness or adequacy of these perceptions.

What struck me at that ritual that provoked these thoughts is that when I alight from or I am about to embark on a flight in Lagos, Dar es Salaam, Accra, or Addis Ababa, I cannot expect to find the equivalent of my greeter. That is, outside of the lucrative high end of our local economies—industry, finance, tourism—African countries do not present attractions for ordinary people who wish to immigrate in search of a better life. And when they do, as is evident in many parts of the continent, they do not win equivalent status such as that of my greeter at the Frankfurt International Airport. They are mostly found in the so-called informal sectors of the economy. It is easy to say that this lack is explained by the prostrate nature of African economies and the endemic instability of African polities. This is too facile a retort, though, and it is not clear to me that it is even plausible. The more plausible explanation must include the fact that Africans do not take citizenship seriously.

Take South Africa, for instance. Since 1994 when the country rid itself of official Apartheid and emplaced a liberal representative multiracial democracy, it has styled itself the "Rainbow Nation." This characterisation is not far-fetched nor is it self-serving. As a result of the Apartheid policies of the past regime in the country and the island of prosperity that it afforded white, including Jewish, immigrants, South Africa attracted all levels of immigrant, non-black populations who sought their fortunes in it. What this means is that, contrary to what might be undeclared but popular wisdom, it cannot be the case that people do not want to come to Africa. White people went to South Africa because they could lead full lives and realise as much of their dreams as their talents, the available resources, and, while Apartheid lasted, their white skins would allow. Apartheid made it even more attractive. Needless to say, people either will not come, or will not stay if they come, if they cannot be promised full citizenship or its equivalent in the lands of their sojourn.

Therein lies the rub: African citizenship is parsimonious, to put it mildly. For the most part, the irony is that African citizenship is redeemed in any serious sense for Africans who travel the world; that is, being the owner of an African passport and travelling on it may be the most rewarding aspect of being a citizen of most African countries. For the rest, the non-responsive and non-responsible character of African governments means most nationals of African countries do not enjoy the most basic privileges of citizenship in their homeland: protection from the predations of their fellows and the overreaching of state functionaries; the provision of basic amenities for the citizens; a minimum standard of living that keeps them above subhuman levels with some luxuries thrown in for good measure; the privilege of having a hand in the constitution of the government that rules them. Above all, pleading lack of resources, African countries are not noted for their quick and adequate protection of their citizens when the latter are victims of oppression and injustice or even natural disasters in other lands. Given what we know of the parsimony of African citizenship across much of the continent, and the sheer absence of it in any but the formal sense in a handful of countries, it would have been a surprise had people thought of Africa as a place where their immigrant restlessness might be accommodated and rewarded; where they and their progeny can look forward to full opportunities to actualise the best and loftiest of their ambitions.

Why would African countries neither take citizenship seriously nor advertise themselves as places where the world can come and realise its dreams of a better life? In a culture dominated by resignation, fatalism, predestination, the widespread belief that "except the Lord buildeth the house, they that do labour in vain," it is clear that the world would be experienced not as a theatre of possibilities, a field of dreams, one in which, in spite of our mortality and the radical inadequacies that attend our best tools, limited only by our imagination or how diligent we are, we can best nurture, build wonderful civilisations and societies in whose culture and abundance the world will come to share and celebrate. I contend that

Africans conceive of the world and experience it in terms of limits, not possibilities; adversity, not advantage; constraints, not opportunities; what is not there, not what is there. In short, the world does not come to Africa and Africans run away from their own continent because African countries are governed by rulers, run by bureaucrats, and guided by intellectuals who are dominated by what I call "the philosophy of limits" as opposed to "the philosophy of possibilities." The philosophy of limits is exemplified in that response that I encounter all too often among African academics every time one comes up with some big challenges to give Africans as good a life as African immigrants chase to the lands of the West.

Here is a concrete example. Ibadan is a huge metropolitan—yes, metropolitan—population centre of more than two million inhabitants. This means that Ibadan is not unlike Toronto or Chicago in terms of its size and, believe it or not, its age. It is a sign of how severely African scholars are ensnared by the picture that, again starting during colonialism, anthropologists have painted of Africa as a place marked by its difference from the rest of the world rather than by its similarity that they think that there is something fabulous about calling a city that came into being in the early nineteenth century "ancient" or "traditional." But styling Ibadan an ancient or a traditional city is the perfect dodge to elide the question of why Toronto and Chicago are far ahead of Ibadan when it comes to modern living and its accoutrements. So when, as I am wont to do, I ask my colleagues why Ibadan does not have a mass transit system—train, tram, and bus; underground, street, and elevated—I almost always receive the refrain: "BUT IT CANNOT BE DONE." I do not exaggerate when I say that this is usually the first answer to my question. The alibis come later.

It is said: where there is a will, there is a way. Having a will translates into not *prima facie* foreclosing any possibility. Often it involves ruling out failure while leaving as the only option the doing of what is on offer. There is no suggestion here that one already has any idea how what the will accepts to do is to be done. But for those imbued with a sense of the possible, who have inculcated the philosophy of possibility, the default response is: IT CAN BE DONE. So they set out to find the appropriate methods—the way—to the destination represented by the challenge they have adopted. Those who are in the grip of the philosophy of limits; who think only or mainly in terms of what they cannot do react differently.

When once you have announced that something cannot be done, it stands to reason that all that you are left with are alibis for your confession of impotence: "We don't have the money." "We don't have the technology." "The West will not let us do it." "Ibadan is a traditional city, and the people will not accept the physical loss of their traditional dwellings that it will take to build the system." "We cannot sustain the cost of running it." And so on. These are all alibis masquerading as explanations. We have seen that these alibis do not avail given the potential of the continent to be a world leader in food, energy, and industrial production.

Now consider an alternative response. Suppose that instead of "it cannot be done" the response is "why not?" or "what a brilliant idea!" Answers of the latter sort bring in their wake ideas, suggestions of what it will take to realise the dream, whether it might be more efficient to segment it into phases, how the many contingencies that arise in its wake might be accommodated and handled, including selling the people on the necessity of the project and the costs it will exact and the impact it will have on their welfare. One cannot overemphasise the importance of this kind of discussion to engaging and energising the citizenry, improving their level of civic education and, as a by-product, the quality of public discourse. It will also draw different groups of experts into such a discourse. But asking for discussions on the wheretos and wherefores of gigantic public works projects cannot but have a salubrious effect on the quality of office holders, even the tenor of political exchanges. Nor should one discount the huge economic prospects—job creation, apprenticeship programmes, manufacturing, supplies, and so on—enfolded by such undertakings. Such discussions will extend into financing and the exigencies of pulling off such a gigantic project.

All who take part in such a discussion will do so for manifold reasons. But all, without exception, must believe that the humanity that resides in Ibadan deserves the best just like their Toronto or Chicago counterparts. It so happens that building for humanity in Ibadan does not mean that only those who live in the immediate vicinity will enjoy the facility when built. By making Ibadan residents more comfortable in their movement and facilitating their business and leisure activities via modern modes of transportation and communication, we are obliquely inviting humanity, both proximate and distant, to come and enjoy a better life even as they work to prosper their lands of sojourn; in this case, in the city of Ibadan. This is why we immigrate to such places as provide these facilities and promise us the possibility of a good life in them.

Such an outcome can only emanate from a philosophy of possibilities informed by a view of human nature that sees Africans not in their difference from, but in their sheer similarity to, the rest of humanity and, for that reason, deserving of the best that human ingenuity can offer. Notice that it is not the concern to attract immigrants that motivates the construction of a modern mass transit system for Ibadan. Rather it is the concern to make "life more abundant" for its resident humanity that is the moving force. Attracting the world and welcoming sojourners from it to Ibadan's gates will be one by-product of taking humanity seriously within its immediate boundaries. When that shall have happened, Ibadan will not only have a modern transit system, it will also have a modern international airport at which those who do the last check of boarding passes and passports of prospective travellers will include Bosnians who speak English and can fully realise their human potential in good modern Ibadan.

INDEX

Olúfẹ́mi Táíwò is Professor of Africana Studies at the Africana Studies and Research Center, Cornell University. He is author of *How Colonialism Preempted Modernity in Africa* (IUP, 2010).

Ingram Content Group UK Ltd.
Milton Keynes UK
UKHW022157220323
419005UK00007B/474